THE ACT OF UNION

BETWEEN THE

EASTERN AND WESTERN CHEROKEES,

THE

CONSTITUTION

AND

AMENDMENTS,

AND THE

LAWS

OF THE

CHEROKEE NATION,

PASSED

DURING THE SESSION OF 1868 AND SUBSEQUENT SESSIONS.

SR Scholarly Resources Inc.
1508 Pennsylvania Avenue · Wilmington, Delaware 19806

SCHOLARLY RESOURCES, INC.
Wilmington, Delaware • London

Reprint edition published in 1975

Library of Congress Catalog Card Number: 75-3669
ISBN: 0-8420-1836-0

Manufactured in the United States of America

THE ACT OF UNION

BETWEEN THE

EASTERN AND WESTERN CHEROKEES,

THE

CONSTITUTION

AND

AMENDMENTS,

AND THE

LAWS

OF THE

CHEROKEE NATION,

PASSED

DURING THE SESSION OF 1868 AND SUBSEQUENT SESSIONS.

TAH-LE-QUAH: CHEROKEE NATION.
NATIONAL PRESS.—EDWIN ARCHER, PRINTER.
1870.

ACT OF UNION

BETWEEN

THE EASTERN AND WESTERN

CHEROKEES.

WHEREAS, our Fathers have existed as a separate and distinct Nation, in the possession and exercise of the essential and appropriate attributes of sovereignty, from a period extending into antiuity, beyond the records and memory of man; *and whereas*, these attributes, with the rights and franchises which they involve, remain still in full force and virtue; as do also the national and social relations of the Cherokee People to each other and to the body politic, excepting in those particulars which have grown out of the provisions of the treaties of 1817 and 1819, between the United States and the Cherokee Nation, under which a portion of our people removed to this country and became a separate community; but the force of circumstances having recently compelled the body of the Eastern Ceerokees to remove to this country, thus bringing together again the two branches of the ancient Cherokee Family; it has become essential to the general welfare that a Union should be formed and a system of Government matured, adapted to their present condition, and providing equally for the protection of each individual in the enjoyment of all his rights.

Therefore, we, the People composing the Eastern and Western Cherokee Nation, in National Convention assembled, by virtue of our original and unalienable rights, do hereby solemnly and mutually agree to form ourselves into one body politic, under the style and title of the CHEROKEE NATION.

In view of thə Uuion now formed, and for the purpose of making satisfactory adjustments of all unsettled business which may have arisen before the consummation of this Union, we agree that such business shall be settled according to the provisions of the respective laws under which it originated, and the Courts of the Cherokee Nation shall be governed in their decisions accordingly. Also, that the Delegation authorized by the Eastern Cherokees to make arrangements with Major General Scott, for their removal to this country, shall continue in charge of that business, with their present powers, until it shall be finally closed. And, also, that all rights and titles to Public Cherokee Lands on the East or West of the River Mississippi, with all other public interests which may have vested in either branch of the Cherokee Family, whether inherited from our Fathers or derived from any other source, shall henceforward vest entire and unimpaired in the Cherokee Nation, as constituted by this Union.

Given under our hands, at Illinois Camp-Ground, this 12th day of July, 1838.

By order of the National Convention:

GEORGE LOWREY,
President of the Eastern Cherokees.
GEORGE GUESS, his x mark,
President of the Western Cherokees

EASTERN CHEROKEES.

R. TAYLOR, V. P.,
JAMES BROWN., V. P.,
TE-KE-CHU-LAS-KEE, V. P.,
GEORGE HICKS,
JOHN BENGE,
THOMAS FOREMAN,
ARCHIBALD CAMPBELL,
JESSE BUSHYHEAD,
LEWIS ROSS,
EDWARD GUNTER,
TE-NAH-LA-WE-STAH,
STEPHEN FOREMAN,
DANIEL McCOY,

By order of the National Convention.

JOHN ROSS,
Principal Chief, Eastern Cherokees,
GOING SNAKE,
Speaker of Council.

WESTERN CHEROKEES.

TOBACCO WILL, V. P.
DAVID MELTON, V. P.,
JOHN DREW, V. P.,
GEORGE BREWER,
THOMAS CANDY,
MOSES PARRIS,
JAMES CAMPBELL,
LOONEY RILEY,
CHARLES GOURD,
LEWIS MELTON,
YOUNG WOLF,
CHARLES COODEY,
AH-STO-LA-TA,
JACK SPEARS,
LOONEY PRICE.

By order of the National Convention.
August 23d, 1839.

JOHN LOONEY, his x mark,
Acting Principal Chief of Western Cherokees.

The foregoing instrument was read, considered, and approved by us, this 23d day of August, 1839.

Aaron Price, Major Pullum, Young Elders, Deer Track, Young Puppy, Turtle Fields, July, The Eagle, The Crying Buffalo; and a great number of respectable Old Settlers and late Emigrants, too numerous to be copied.

THE
CONSTITUTION
OF THE
CHEROKEE NATION.

The Eastern and Western Cherokees having again re-united, and become one body politic, under the style and title of the Cherokee Nation: *Therefore*,

We, the people of the Cherokee Nation, in National Convention assembled, in order to establish justice, insure tranquility, promote the common welfare, and to secure to ourselves and our posterity the blessings of freedom—acknowledging, with humility and gratitude, the goodness of the Sovereign Ruler of the Universe in permitting us so to do, and imploring His aid and guidance in its accomplishment—do ordain and establish this Constitution for the government of the Cherokee Nation.

Article I.

Sec. 1. The boundary of the Cherokee Nation shall be that described in the treaty of 1833 between the United States and Western Cherokees, subject to such extension as may be made in the adjustment of the unfinished business with the United States.

Sec. 2. The lands of the Cherokee Nation shall remain common property; but the improvements made thereon, and in the possession of the citizens of the Nation, are the exclusive and indefeasible property of the citizens respectively who made, or may rightfully be in possession of them: *Provided*, That the citizens of the Nation possessing exclusive and indefeasible right to their improvements, as expressed in this article, shall possess no right or power to dispose of their improvements, in any manner whatever, to the United States, individual States, or to individual citizens thereof; and that, whenever any citizen shall remove with his effects out of the limits of this Nation, and become a citizen of any other Government, all his rights and privileges as a citizen of this Nation shall cease: *Provided, nevertheless*, That the National Council shall have power to re-admit, by law, to all the rights of citizenship, any such person or persons who may, at any time, desire to return to the Nation, on memorializing the National Council for such re-admission.

Moreover, the National Council shall have power to adopt such laws and regulations as its wisdom may deem expedient and proper to prevent citizens from monopolizing improvements with the view of speculation.

Article II.

Sec. 1. The power of this Government shall be divided into three distinct departments:—the Legislative, the Executive, and the Judicial.

Sec. 2. No person or persons belonging to one of these departments shall exercise any of the powers properly belonging to either of the others, except in the cases hereinafter expressly directed or permitted.

Article III.

Sec. 1. The Legislative power shall be vested in two distinct branches:—a National Committee and Council; and the style of their acts shall be:—*Be it enacted by the National Council.*

Sec. 2. The National Council shall make provision, by law, for laying off the Cherokee Nation into Eight Districts; and, if subsequently it should be deemed expedient, one or two may be added thereto.

Sec. 3. The National Committee shall consist of two members from each District, and the Council shall consist of three members from each District, to be chosen by the qualified electors in their respective Districts for two years; the elections to be held in the respective Districts every two years, at such times and places as may be directed by law.

The National Council shall, after the present year, be held annually, to be convened on the first Monday in October, at such place as may be designated by the National Council, or, in case of emergency, by the Principal Chief.

Sec. 4. Before the Districts shall be laid off, any election which may take place shall be by general vote of the electors throughout the Nation for all officers to be elected.

The first election for all the officers of the Government:—Chiefs, Executive Council, Members of the National Council, Judges and Sheriffs,—shall be held at Tah-Le-Quah, before the rising of this Convention; and the term of service of all officers elected previous to the First Monday in October, 1839, shall be extended to embrace, in addition to the regular Constitutional Term, the time intervening from their election to the First Monday in October, 1839.

Sec. 5. No person shall be eligible to a seat in the National Council but a free Cherokee Male Citizen, who shall have attained to the age of twenty-five years.

The descendants of Cherokee men by all free women, except the African Race, whose parents may have been living together as man and wife, according to the customs and laws of this Nation, shall be entitled to all the rights and privileges of this Nation, as well as the posterity of Cherokee women by all free men. No person who is of negro or mulatto parentage, either by the father's or the mother's side, shall be eligible to hold any office of profit, honor, or trust under this Government

Sec. 6. The Electors and Members of the National Council shall in all cases, except those of treason, felony, or breach of the peace, be privileged from arrest during their attendance at elections, and at the National Council, in going to and returning.

Sec. 7. In all Elections by the People, the Electors shall vote *viva voce*.

All Free Male Citizens, who shall have attained to the age of eighteen years shall be equally entitled to vote at all Public Elections.

Sec. 8. Each Branch of the National Council shall judge of the qualifications and returns of its own members; and determine the Rules of its Proceedings; punish a Member for disorderly behaviour; and, with the concurrence of two-thirds, expel a Member; but not a second time for the same offence.

SEC. 9. Each Branch of the National Council, when assembled, shall choose its own officers; a majority of each shall constitute a quorum to do business, but a smaller number may adjourn from day to day and compel the attendance of absent members, in such manner and under such penalty as each Branch may prescribe.

SEC. 10. The Members of the National Committee shall each receive from the Public Treasury a compensation for their services which shall be three dollars per day during their attendance at the National Council; and the Members of the Council shall each receive three dollars per day for their services during their attendance at the National Council, provided that the same may be increased or diminished by law; but no alteration shall take effect during the period of service of the Members of the National Council by whom such alteration may have been made.

SEC. 11. The National Council shall regulate by law, by whom and in what manner, Writs of Elections shall be issued to fill the vacancies which may happen in either branch thereof.

SEC. 12. Eeach Member of the National Council, before he takes his seat, shall take the following oath, or affirmation:—**I, A. B.,** do solemnly swear, (or affirm; as the case may be); that I have not obtained my election by bribery, treats, or any undue and unlawful means, used by myself or others by my desire or approbation for that purpose;—that I consider myself constitutionally qualified as a member of ———; and that on all questions and measures which may come before me I will so give my vote and so conduct myself as in my judgment shall appear most conducive to the interest and prosperity of this Nation, and that I will bear true faith and allegiance to the same, and to the utmost of my ability and power observe, conform to, support and defend the Constitution thereof.

SEC. 13. No person who may be convicted of felony shall be eligible to any office or appointment of honor, profit, or trust within this Nation.

SEC. 14. The National Council shall have power to

make all Laws and Regulations which they shall deem necessary and proper for the good of the Nation, which shall not be contrary to this Constitution.

SEC. 15. It shall be the duty of the National Council to pass such Laws as may be necessary and proper to decide dfferences by arbitration, to be appointed by the parties who may choose that summary mode of adjustment.

SEC. 16. No power of suspending the laws of this Nation shall be exercised, unless by the National Council or its authority.

SEC. 17. No Retrospective Law, nor any Law impairing the Obligation of Contracts, shall be passed.

SEC. 18. The National Council shall have power to make Laws for Laying and Collecting Taxes, for the purpose of Raising a Revenue.

SEC. 19. All Bills making Appropriations shall originate in the National Committee, but the Council may propose Amendments or reject the same. All other Bills may originate in either Branch, subject to the concurrence or rejection of the other.

SEC. 20. All Acknowledged Treaties shall be the Supreme Law of the Land, and the National Council shall have the sole power of deciding on the construction of all Treaty Stipulations.

SEC. 21. The Council shall have the sole power of Impeaching. All Impeachments shall be tried by the National Committee. When Sitting for that purpose the Member shall be upon oath or affirmation; and no person shall be convicted without the concurrence of two-thirds of the Members present.

SEC. 22. The Principal Chief, Assistant Principal Chief, and all Civil Officers, shall be liable to Impeachment for misdemeanor in office; but judgment in such cases shall not extend further than Removal from Office and Disqualification to hold any Offiice of Honor, Trust, or Profit under the Government of this Nation.

The Party, whether convicted or acquitted, shall, nevertheless, be liable to indictment, trial, judgment and punishment according to law.

Article IV.

Sec. 1. The Supreme Executive Power of this Nation shall be vested in a Principal Chief, who shall be styled the Principal Chief of the Cherokee Nation.

The Principal Chief shall hold his Office for the Term of Four Years; and shall be Elected by the Qualified Electors on the same day and at the places where they shall respectively vote for Members of the National Council.

The Returns of the Election for Principal Chief shall be Sealed Up and directed to the President of the National Committee, who shall Open and Publish them in the Presence of the National Council Assembled. The Person having the Highest Number of Votes shall be Principal Chief; but if Two or more shall be Equal and Highest in Votes, one of them shall be Chosen by Joint Vote of Both Branches of the Council. The manner of determining Contested Elections shall be directed by Law.

Sec. 2. No Person except a Natural Born Citizen shall be Eligible to the Office of Principal Chief; neither shall any Person be Eligible to that Office who shall not have attained to the age of Thirty-Five Years.

Sec. 3. There shall also be Chosen at the same time, by the Qualified Electors in the same manner for Four Years, an Assistant Principal Chief, who shall have attained to the age of Thirty-Five Years.

Sec. 4. In case of the Removal of the Principal Chief from Office, or of his Death or Resignation, or Inability to Discharge the Powers and Duties of the said Office, the same shall devolve on the Assistant Principal Chief until the Disability be removed or the Vacancy filled by the National Council.

Sec. 5. The National Council may by Law provide for the case of Removal, Death, Resignation, or Disability of both the Principal and Assistant Principal Chief, declaring what Officer shall then act as Principal Chief until the Disability be removed or a Principal Chief shall be Elected.

Sec. 6. The Principal Chief and Assistant Principal Chief shall, at stated times, receive for their Services a Compensation, which shall neither be increased nor diminished during the period for which they shall have been elected; and they shall not receive within that period any other emolument from the Cherokee Nation or any other Government

SEC. 7. Before the Principal Chief enters upon the execution of his office, he shall take the following oath or affirmation:—

"I do solemnly swear, or affirm, that I will faithfully execute the duties of Principal Chief of the Cherokee Nation, and will, to the best of my ability, preserve, protect, and defend the Constitution of the Cherokee Nation."

SEC. 8. He may, on extraordinary occasions, convene the National Council at the Seat of Government.

SEC. 9. He shall, from time to time, give to the National Council information of the state of the Government, and recommend to their consideration such measures as he may deem expedient.

SEC. 10. He shall take care that the laws be faithfully executed.

SEC. 11. It shall be his duty to visit the different Districts, at least, once in two years, to inform himself of the general condition of the country.

SEC. 12. The Assistant Principal Chief shall, by virtue of his office, aid and advise the Principal Chief in the Administration of the Government at all times during his continuance in office.

SEC. 13. Vacancies that may occur in offices, the appointment of which is vested in the National Council, shall be filled by the Principal Chief, during the Recess of the National Council, by granting Commissions which shall expire at the end of the next Session thereof.

SEC. 14. Every Bill which shall pass both Branches of the National Council shall, before it becomes a Law, be presented to the Principal Chief; if he approve, he shall sign it, but if not, he shall return it, with his objections, to that Branch in which it may have originated, who shall enter the objections at large on their journals, and proceed to reconsider it; if, after such reconsideration, two-thirds of that Branch shall agree to pass the Bill, it shall be sent, together with the objections, to the other Branch, by which it shall likewise be reconsidered, and if approved by two-thirds of that

Branch, it shall become a law. If any Bill shall not be returned by the Principal Chief within five days, (Sundays excepted), after the same has been presented to him, it shall become a law, in like manner as if he had signed it; unless the National Council, by their adjournment, prevent its return; in which case it shall be a law, unless sent back within three days after their next meeting.

SEC. 15. Members of the National Council, and all Officers, Executive and Judicial, shall be Bound by Oath to Support the Constitution of this Nation, and to Perform the Duties of their Respective Offices with Fidelity.

SEC. 16. In case of disagreement between the two Branches of the National Council, with respect to the time of adjournment, the Principal Chief shall have power to adjourn the same to such time as he may deem proper; *Provided*, it be not a period beyond the next Constitutional Meeting thereof.

SEC. 17. The Principal Chief shall, during the Session of the National Council, attend at the Seat of Government.

SEC. 18. There shall be a Council composed of Five Persons, to be appointed by the National Council, whom the Principal Chief shall have full power, at his discretion, to assemble. He, together with the Assistant Principal Chief, and the Councillors, or a Majority of them, may, from time to time, hold and keep a Council for ordering and directing the affairs of the Nation according to law; *Proviedd*, the National Council shall have power to reduce the number, if deemed expedient, after the first term of service, to a number not less than three.

SEC. 19. The Members of the Executive Council shall be chosen for the Term of Two Years.

SEC. 20. The Resolutions and Advice of the Council shall be Recorded in a Register and Signed by the Members agreeing thereto, which may be called for by either Branch of the National Council, and any Councillor may enter his dissent to the Majority.

SEC. 21. The Treasurer of the Cherokee Nation shall be Chosen by a Joint Vote of Both Branches of the National Council for a Term of Four Years.

SEC. 22. The Treasurer shall, before entering upon the

Duties of his Office, give Bond to the Nation, with Sureties to the satisfaction of the National Council, for the Faithful Discharge of his Trust.

SEC. 23. No Money shall be Drawn from the Treasury but by Warrant from the Principal Chief, and in consequence of Appropriations made by Law.

SEC. 24. It shall be the Duty of the Treasurer to Receive All Public Moneys, and to Make a Regular Statement and Account of the Receipts and Expenditures of All Public Moneys at the Annual Session of the National Council.

ARTICLE V.

SEC. 1. The Judicial Powers shall be Vested in a Supreme Court, and such Circuit and Inferior Courts as the National Council may, from time to time, Ordain and Establish.

SEC. 2. The Judges of the Supreme and Circuit Courts shall hold their Commissions for the Term of Four Years; but any of them may be Removed From Office, on the Address of Two-Thirds of Each Branch of the National Council to the Principal Chief for that purpose.

SEC. 3. The Judges of the Supreme and Circuit Courts shall, at Stated Times, Receive a Compensation which shall not be Diminished during their Continuance In Office; but they shall Receive No Fees or Perquisites of Office, nor hold any other Office of Profit or Trust under the Government of this Nation or any other Power.

SEC. 4. No Person shall be appointed a Judge of any of the Courts until he shall have attained to the Age of Thirty Years.

SEC. 5. The Judges of the Supreme and Circuit Courts shall be Elected by the National Council, and there shall be appointed in Each District as many Justices of the Peace as it may be deemed expedient for the Public Good; whose Powers, Duties, and Duration In Office, shall be clearly Designated by Law.

SEC. 6. The Judges of the Supreme Court and of the Circuit Courts shall have Complete Criminal Jurisdiction in such Cases and in such Manner as may be pointed out by Law.

SEC. 7. No Judge shall Sit on Trial of any Cause when the Parties are Connected by Affinity or Consanguinity, except by Consent of the Parties.

In case All the Judges of the Supreme Court shall be Interested in the Issue of any Cause, or Related to all or either of the Parties, the National Council may Provide by Law for the Selection of a Suitable Number of Persons, of Good Character and Knowledge, for the Determination thereof, and who shall be Specially Commissioned for the Adjudication of such Case by the Principal Chief.

SEC. 8. All Writs, and other Process, shall run: "*In the Name of the Cherokee Nation*"; and bear Test and be Signed by the Respective Clerks.

SEC. 9. Indictments shall conclude:—"*Against the Peace and Dignity of the Cherokee Nation*".

SEC. 10. The Supreme Court shall, after the Present Year, Hold its Session Annually at the Seat of Government; to be Convened on the First Monday of October, in Each Year.

SEC. 11. In all Criminal Prosecutions, the Accused shall have the Right of being Heard; of Demanding the Nature and Cause of the Accusation; of Meeting the Witnesses face to face; of having Compulsory Process for obtaining Witnesses in his or their Favor; and in Prosecutions by Indictment or Information, a Speedy Public Trial, by an Impartial Jury of the Vicinage; nor shall the Accused be Compelled to Give Evidence against himself.

SEC. 12. The People shall be Secure in their Persons, Houses, Papers, and Possessions, from Unreasonable Seizures and Searches; and No Warrant to Search Any Place, or to Seize any Person or Things, shall Issue without Describing them as nearly as may be, nor without Good Cause, Supported by Oath or Affirmation.

SEC. 13. All Persons shall be Bailable by Sufficient Securities, unless for Capital Offences, where the Proof is Evident, or Presumption Great.

ARTICLE VI.

SEC. 1. No Person who Denies the being of a God, or a

Future State of Reward and Punishment, shall Hold any Office in the Civil Department in this Nation.

SEC. 2. The Free Exercise of Religious Worship, and Serving God without distinction, shall, Forever, Be Enjoyed within the Limits of this Nation; *Provided*, that this Liberty of Conscience shall not be so Construed as to excuse Acts of Licentiousness, or Justify Practices Inconsistent with the Peace or Safety of this Nation.

SEC. 3. When the National Council shall determine the expediency of Appointing Delegates, or other Public Agents, for the purpose of transacting business with the Government of the United States, the Principal Chief shall recommend, and, by the Advice and Consent of the National Committee, Appoint and Commission such Delegates, or Public Agents, accordingly. On all matters of interest, touching the Rights of the Citizens of this Nation, which may require the attention of the United States Government, the Principal Chief shall keep up a Friendly Correspondence with that Government, through the medium of its Proper Officers.

SEC. 4. All Commissions shall be:—"*In the Name and by the Authority of the Cherokee Nation;*" and be Sealed with the Seal of the Nation, and Signed by the Principal Chief. The Principal Chief shall make use of his Private Seal until a National Seal shall be Provided.

SEC. 5. A Sheriff shall be Elected in Each District, by the Qualified Electors thereof, who shall Hold his Office Two Years, unless Sooner Removed. Should a Vacancy occur, Subsequent to an Election, it shall be Filled by the Principal Chief, as in other cases; and the Person so Appointed, shall Continue in Office until the next Regular Election.

SEC. 6. No Person shall, for the same offence, be Twice put in Jeopardy of Life or Limb; nor shall the Property of any person be Taken and Applied to Public Use without a just and Fair Compensation: *Provided*, That nothing in this clause shall be so Construed as to Impair the Right and Power of the National Council to lay and Collect Taxes.

SEC. 7. The Right of Trial by Jury, shall remain Inviolate, and every person, for Injury Sustained in Person,

Property, or Reputation, shall have Remedy by due Course of Law.

Sec. 8. The Appointment of All Officers, not otherwise Directed by this Constitution, shall be Vested in the National Council.

Sec. 9. Religion, Morality, and Knowledge, being necessary to Good Government, the Preservation of Liberty and the Happiness of Mankind; Schools, and the Means of Education, Shall Forever be Encouraged in this Nation.

Sec. 10. The National Council may Propose such Amendments to this Constitution, as Two-Thirds of Each Branch may deem Expedient; and the Principal Chief shall Issue a Proclamation, Directing all Civil Officers of the Several Districts to Promulgate the same as extensively as possible within their respective Districts, at least Six Months Previous to the Next General Election. And if, at the First Session of the National Council, after such General Election, Two-Thirds of Each Branch shall, by Ayes and Noes, ratify such Proposed Amendments, they shall be Valid, to all Intent and Purposes, as Parts of this Constitution: *Provided*, That such Proposed Amendments shall be Read on Three Several Days in Each Branch, as well when the same are Proposed, as when they are Ratified.

Done in Convention: at Tah-Le-Quah, Cherokee Nation, This Sixth Day of September, 1839.

GEORGE LOWREY,
President of the National Convention.

Hair Conrad, his x mark,
John Benge, his x mark,
Archibald Campbell, his x mark,
Thomas Candy, John Drew,
George Guess, his x mark,
Walter Scott Adair,
Young Elders, his x mark,
Will. Shorey Coodey,
Thomas Foreman, Richard Taylor,
Thomas Fox Taylor,
O-kan-sto-tah Logan, his x mark,
James Spears, his x mark,
John Spears,
Stephen Foreman,
Young Glass, his x mark,
Looney Price,
Tobacco Will, his x mark,
Major Pullum, his x mark,
Moses Parris,
George Washington Gunter,

Kenah Logan, his x mark,
Young Wolf, Joseph Martin Lynch,
Sal-la-tee-skee Watts, his x mark,
George Brewer, his x mark,
Joshua Buffington,
Jesse Bushyhead, Jesse Russell,
John Fletcher Boot, his x mark,
Crying Buffalo, his x mark,
Bark Flute, his x mark,
Oo-la-yo-a, his x mark,
Soft-Shell Turtle, his x mark,
Edward Gunter,
Daniel Colston, his x mark,
Lewis Ross, George Hicks,
Turtle Fields, his x mark,
Elijah Hicks,
Tah-lah-see-nee, his x mark,
James Brown, Charles Coodey,
Riley Keys, Daniel McCoy,
Lewis Melton,

PROCLAMATION

AND

AMENDMENTS

TO THE

CONSTITUTION:

Adopted November 26th, 1866.

PROCLAMATION BY THE PRINCIPAL CHIEF.

WHEREAS, The National Council adopted certain amendments to the Constitution of the Cherokee Nation, and submitted the same to a general convention of the people of the Cherokee Nation, called at Tahlequah, on the 26th day of November, A. D. 1866, and which said amendments, with the Preamble thereto attached, were in the following words, to wit:

WHEREAS, By the treaty executed at Washington, on the 19th day of July, A. D. 1866, between the United States and the Cherokee Nation, through its delegation, ratified by the Senate and officially promulgated by the President of the United States, August 11th, 1866, certain things were agreed to between the parties to said treaty, involving changes in the Constitution of the Cherokee Nation, which changes can not be accomplished by the usual mode, and

WHEREAS, It is the desire of the people and Government of the Cherokee Nation, to carry out in good faith all of its obligations, to the end that law and order be preserved, and the institutions of their government maintained,

Therefore, be it resolved by the National Council, That the following amendments to the Constitution of the Cherokee Nation be submitted to a convention of the Cherokee people, to assemble at Tahlequah, on the twenty-sixth (26th) day of November A. D. 1866, under the Proclamation of the Principal Chief, and should said amendments hereunto annexed, be ratified by said convention, then they shall be officially published and declared by the Principal Chief to be, and shall constitute a part or parts of the Constitution of the Cherokee Nation.

AMENDMENTS.

Amendments to Article I.

Sec. 1. The boundary of the Cherokee Nation shall be that described in the treaty of 1833, between the United States and the Western Cherokees, subject to such modification as may be made necessary by the 17th article of the treaty concluded at Washington City, on the 19th day of July, 1866, between the United States and the Cherokee Nation.

Sec. 2. The lands of the Cherokee Nation shall remain Common Property until the National Council shall request the survey and allotment of the same, in accordance with the provisions of article 20th of the treaty of 19th of July, 1866, between the United States and the Cherokee Nation.

Amendments to Article III.

Sec. 1. The Upper House of the National Council, known as the National Committee, shall be hereafter known and styled the Senate of the Cherokee Nation, and shall consist of Two Senators for every District in the Cherokee Nation.

SEC. 2. The Council shall consist of Two Members from each District, and when a District shall have to exceed Two Hundred Voters, it shall have an Additional Member, and for every Additional Two Hundred Voters in said District, upwards of Four Hundred, it shall have an Additional Member. *Provided*, That when any District shall have less than One Hundréd Voters according to the Census, it shall still be entitled to One Representative.

SEC. 3. In order to ascertain and fix the Representation to the Council, provided for by the preceding section, the National Council shall cause to be taken as soon as practicable, a Census of the Population of the Cherokee Nation, according to Districts. A Second Census shall be taken in like manner, in the year 1870, and each Ten Years thereafter, and the National Council shall Regularly Apportion Representation among the Several Districts, as Provided in the Preceding Section, agreeably to such Census. The First Apportionment, provided for above, shall be made before the First Day of June, and shall govern the Election to be held on the First Monday in August, 1867.

SEC. 4. The National Council shall, after the present year be held Annually, to be Convened on the First Monday in November, at such place as may be designated by the National Council, or in case of emergency by the Principal Chief.

SEC. 5. No Person shall be Eligible to a Seat in the National Council but a Male Citizen of the Cherokee Nation, who shall have attained to the age of Twenty-Five Years, and who shall have been a *bona fide* Resident of the District in which he may be Elected, at least Six Months immediately preceding such Election. All Native Born Cherokees, all Indians and Whites Legally Members of the Nation by Adoption, and all Freedmen who have been Liberated by Voluntary Act of their Former Owners or by Law, as well as Free Colored Persons who were in the Country at the Commencement of the Rebellion, and are now Residents therein, or who may Return within Six Months from the 19th day of July, 1866, and their Descendants, who Reside within the Limits of the Cherokee Nation, shall be taken, and deemed to be Citizens of the Cherokee Nation.

Sec. 6. The Members of the National Council shall each receive from the Public Treasury a Compensation for their Services, which shall be Three Dollars Per Day during their attendance at the National Council upon any Regular Session, not exceeding Thirty Days; *Provided*, That the Per Diem allowance may be Increased or Diminished by Law; but no Alteration shall take effect during the Period of Service of the Members of the National Council, by whom such Alteration may have been made.

Sec. 7. All Male Citizens, who have attained the age of Eighteen Years, shall be deemed Qualified Electors of the Cherokee Nation; and there shall be no Restrictions by Law, save such as are required for persons convicted of crime, or for such limit as to residence, not exceeding Six Months in the District where the Vote is offered, as may be required by Census or Registration.

Amendments to Article V.

Sec. 1. The Supreme Court shall consist of Three Judges, who shall be Elected by the National Council, and whose Duties, Jurisdiction, and Compensation shall be Defined by Law, in the manner prescribed by the Constitution. The National Council, at its Annual Session in 1867, shall Elect One of the Supreme Judges for Three Years, One for Two Years, and One for One Year; and at each Annual Session of the National Council thereafter shall Elect One Supreme Judge, whose Official Term shall be Three Years.

Sec. 2. The Judges of the Circuit Court shall hereafter be Elected by the People, for the Term of Four Years, and shall have the same Jurisdiction, Discharge the same Duties, and be Compensated in the same manner, as is now Provided for by the Constitution. There shall be Elected in like manner, in and for Each District, as many Judges as it may be deemed Expedient for the Public Good, whose Powers, Duties, and Duration in Office, shall be clearly Designated by Law.

Article VII.

Sec. 1. Neither Slavery nor Involuntary Servitude shall

ever hereafter exist in the Cherokee Nation, otherwise than in the Punishment of Crime, whereof the Party shall have been duly Convicted; and any Provision of the Constitution of the Cherokee Nation Conflicting with the foregoing section, is hereby Annulled.

SEC. 2. The Persons now holding Office shall Continue therein, except, as may be otherwise expressly Provided by Law for Canadian District, until their Successors be Commissioned in November, 1867.

TAH-LE-QUAH, CHEROKEE NATION,
November, 29*th*, 1866.

SMITH CHRISTIE,
President of National Committee.

Concurred:

WRITER,
Speaker of Council.

Approved:

WILL. P. ROSS.

At a General Convention of the People of the Cherokee Nation, held at Tah-le-quah, Cherokee Nation, on the 28th day of November, A. D. 1866, for the purpose of taking into consideration the Foregoing Amendments to the Constitution of the Cherokee Nation; and whereof Riley Keys, Chief Justice of the Supreme Court, was chosen President, and Budd Gritts, Secretary: The said Amendments to the Constitution of the Cherokee Nation were Read, Considered, and severally Approved and Adopted by the Cherokee People.

In Testimony Whereof, the President and Secretary of said Convention have Subscribed the same at Tah-le-quah, Cherokee Nation, on this the 28th day of November, A. D. 1866.

RILEY KEYS,
President of the Convention.
BUDD GRITTS,
Secretary.

AND WHEREAS: The said Foregoing Amendments to the Constitution were duly submitted to the said General Convention of the Cherokee People; and were severally Read, Considered, and Adopted on the 28th day of November, A. D. 1866.

Now, Therefore, Be it known, that I, William P. Ross, Principal Chief of the Cherokee Nation, do Issue this, my Proclamation, Declaring said Amendments to be a Part of the Constitution of the Cherokee Nation. In Testimony Whereof I have hereunto Subscribed my Name: This, the 7th day of December, A. D. 1866.

WILL. P. ROSS,
Principal Chief.

LAWS

OF THE

CHEROKEE NATION.

Resolution in relation to the Postponement of Opening Election Returns.

WHEREAS, The Second Monday of November being the day fixed on, by [an] Act passed September 28, 1868, when the Election Returns of Delegates to the Grand Council are to be opened by the President of the Senate, in presence of both Houses of the National Council; and,

WHEREAS, The Returns from Going Snake District have not been made; therefore, be it

Resolved by the National Council, That the opening of the Election Returns be postponed until Monday next, the 16th instant; and that the Principal Chief be requested to order the Sheriff of the said Going Snake District to have the Returns of the said District at Tahlequah, without failure, on that day.

Approved: LEWIS DOWNING, *Principal Chief C. N.*
Tahlequah, C. N., Nov. 9, 1868.

An Act Making Appropriations for Special Services rendered by the Persons Named in the Account.

THE CHEROKEE NATION, DR.

To Young Pig, 9 days, at $3 per day, -	$27 00
" Josh. Ross, 7 days, at $3 per day, -	21 00
" John McIntosh, 5 days, at $3 per day,	15 00
" William Cochran, 3 days, as guide and messenger, at $3 per day, - - - -	9 00
" Alex. Hawk, Interpreter, 3 days, at $3 per day, - - - - - - -	9 00
	$81 00

Be it enacted by the National Council, That the sum of Eighty-One Dollars be, and the same is hereby appropriated, out of any money in the Treasury, belonging to the General Fund, not otherwise appropriated, for the use and benefit of the foregoing named persons, according to the amounts set opposite each person's name; and the Principal Chief is hereby authorized to draw warrants for the same.

Approved: LEWIS DOWNING,
Principal Chief of the Cherokee Nation.
Tahlequah, C. N., Nov. 11, 1868.

An Act Making an Appropriation for the Benefit of Martin McCoy, Jas. Trott, (or Badger,) and Joseph Coody.

Be it enacted by the National Council, That the sum of Two Hundred and Forty-Nine Dollars and Twenty-Five Cents, ($249.25), be, and the same is hereby appropriated, out of any funds in the National Treasury, belonging to the General Fund, not otherwise appropriated, for the benefit of Martin McCoy, Jas. Trott, (or Badger,) and Joseph Coody, as follows:

For Martin McCoy, - - - - - -	$ 91 25
" Jas. Trott, (or Badger,) - - - -	128 00
" Joseph Coody, - - - - -	30 00

And the Principal Chief will be authorized to issue warrants accordingly.

Approved: LEWIS DOWNING,
Principal Chief of the Cherokee Nation.
Tahlequah, C. N., Nov. 13, 1868.

An Act in reference to the Delawares and Osages.

Be it enacted by the National Council, That the Principal Chief be and he is hereby authorized to appoint two suitable Commissioners, at his earliest convenience, whose duty it shall be to proceed at once to the Delawares, in Coo-wee-scoo-wee District, and lay before them, (or their Chief, if any there be,) a copy of a communication received by the late Cherokee Delegation, from the Hon. Commissioner of Indian Affairs, at Washington, dated August 7th, 1868; and to ascertain whether or not the said Delawares have completed and filed in the Office of Indian Affairs, at Washington, their Census Rolls, as contemplated by the agreement made between them and the Cherokees, at Washinton, on the 8th day of April, A. D. 1867. And if the said Delawares have not completed and transmitted their said "Census Rolls," then the said Commissioners will be authorized to urge them to do so, at their earliest convenience, to the end that the Cherokees may receive the funds due them, under the said arrangement between them and the Cherokees.

Be it further enacted, That the said Commissioners shall proceed to the Osages, and notify them, (through their authorities) that their depredations upon the Delawares and other Cherokee citizens must cease at once, and that they (the Osages) are required to return, at the earliest practicable moment, all stock, of every kind, that they have stolen, or taken from the Delawares, or other Cherokees; and that, should they (the Osages) fail or refuse to return such stock, that they will be reported to the Government of the United States, and reparation and indemnity will be demanded for all depredations committed by them, under the 26th Article of the Treaty of 1866, made between the Cherokees and the United States.

Be it further enacted, That the said Commissioners shall be paid at the rate of three dollars per day, for every day actually employed in the duties of the said Commission, payable out of any funds belonging to the National Fund, not otherwise appropriated, in the National Treasury, on their certified account; and the Principal Chief is hereby authorized to draw warrants for the same. This act to take effect from and after its passage.

Approved: LEWIS DOWNING,
Principal Chief of the Cherokee Nation.
Tahlequah, C. N., Nov. 14, 1868.

An Act creating a Commission to Investigate Claims to Town Lots, Buildings, &c., and other matters, in Fort Gibson and Tahlequah.

Be it enacted by the National Council, That a Commission, composed of two persons, be appointed by the Principal Chief, whose duty it shall be to ascertain the names of all the original purchasers of Town Lots at Fort Gibson and Tahlequah; the present holders and claimants of the said Lots and Buildings, which have been sold; the amounts respectively for which the Lots and Buildings were sold by the Nation; the amount which has been paid upon each purchase, or bid; and the amounts remaining unpaid, and yet due, from each purchaser, owner, or claimant, to the Cherokee Nation.

Said Commission shall sit at Fort Gibson, or Tahlequah, according to their convenience, or the requirements of their business, during the month of February, 1869. For the more thorough performance of their duties, the said Commissioners are hereby authorized and empowered to call for books, papers, plats, &c., in relation to the said Towns, and Town Lots thereof; to administer oaths; to take parol and documentary evidence in regard to the said Town Lots, and Lots and Buildings, for the discovery of all important facts, connected with, and serving to exhibit the true condition of the same, as set forth above.

The said Commissioners are likewise required to keep a correct record of their proceedings, from day to day, while in service, and report the facts elicited in regard to each claim on Lots, &c., separately, with the evidence taken, and their action thereon, to the next Session of the National Council.

Be it further enacted, That at the expiration of the Session of the said Commissioners, they are required to notify, by the most practicable and convenient means, each proper purchaser, assign, or claimant, of Lots and Buildings, yet remaining in part unpaid for, the amount found due the Cherokee Nation from such proper purchaser, assign, or claimant, by said Commissioners.

And all persons who may be found by said Commissioners, under authority of this act, to owe the Cherokee Nation any installment, or installments, or any portion thereof, are hereby required to pay the full amount of the sum so due, to the National Treasurer, within six months from the first day of March, 1869. And upon failure of any person indebted to the Nation, in the amount ascertained and adjudged against him, or her, by the said Commissioners, [they] shall forfeit all right to the Lots not wholly paid for, and the said Town Lot, or Lots and Buildings, shall revert to the Nation, and be subject to be sold again to the highest bidder. *Provided*, That nothing in this act shall shall be so construed as conferring authority upon said Commissioners to settle a question of right to Town Lots, or Lots and Buildings, between two or more contending parties, each claiming the same property.

Be it further enacted, That the said Commissioners be allowed three dollars per day, each, while in actual service.

Be it further enacted, That the Commissioners provided for in this act, before they enter upon the duties required of them, shall take the following oath: "I do solemnly swear that I will, to the best of my ability and skill, and without partiality or affection, faithfully discharge the duties required of me in the foregoing act."

PIG SMITH,
President of Senate.

Concurred in: JOHN YOUNG,
Speaker of Council.

Approved: LEWIS DOWNING,
Principal Chief of the Cherokee Nation.

Tahlequah, C. N., Nov. 18, 1868.

An Act Approving of the Agreement made with the Munsee, or Christian Indians, of Kansas.

Articles of Agreement, made and entered into this Sixth day of August, A. D. 1868, between the Cherokee Nation of Indians, represented by the following duly authorized Delegates and Representatives, viz:—Lewis Downing, Principal Chief; H. D. Reese, Chairman; W. P. Adair, J. P. Davis, E. C. Boudinot, Arch. Scraper, Samuel Smith, and J. A. Scales; and the Munsee, or Christian Indians, of Kansas, represented by their duly authorized Councilmen, Ignatius Caleb, and Moses Kilbuck—

WITNESSETH: That the said Cherokee Nation, actuated by motives of humanity, and a sincere desire to do good to all civilized Indians, hereby agree to receive said Munsee, or Christian Indians, into the Cherokee Nation, and to confer upon them all the rights and privileges of Cherokee citizens; and the said Munsee, or Christian Indians, by their Representatives, as aforesaid, hereby agree to abide by, conform to, and obey the Constitution and Laws of the Cherokee Nation,

In consideration whereof, the said Munsee, or Christian Indians, by their Representatives, agree to pay to said Cherokee Nation, to become a part of the National Fund of said Cherokee Nation, the sum of Four Thousand Dollars, (this being the amount of available means for that purpose,) the same to be paid within sixty days after the Treaty concluded between the United States and said Munsee, or Christian Indians, June 1, 1868, shall have been ratified by the Senate of the United States.

It is hereby agreed further, by and between the parties hereto, that the consent of the Cherokee National Council shall be procured for the use and occupancy, by a Missionary for the Munsees, or Christian Indians, of a quantity of land; not exceeding one hundred and sixty acres, in the Cherokee country, in accordance with the provisions of the fourteenth article of the Treaty concluded between the Cherokees and the United States, July 19, 1866.

In testimony whereof, the parties hereto have set our hands and seals, the day and year first above written.

LEWIS DOWNING,	L. S.
H. D. REESE,	L. S.
W. P. ADAIR.	L. S.
SAMUEL SMITH,	L. S.
ARCH. SCRAPER,	L. S.
J. PORUM DAVIS,	L. S.
E. C. BOUDINOT,	L. S.
J. A. SCALES,	L. S.
IGNATIUS CALEB,	L. S.
MOSES KILBUCK.	L. S.

WITNESSES:
WILLIAM HAYES,
EDM. F. BROWN.

Be it enacted by the National Council, That the foregoing agreement, made and entered into between the Cherokees and the Munsees, or Christian Indians, be, and the same is hereby approved and ratified, by striking out the clause providing for a Missionary Reservation.

JOHN YOUNG,
Speaker of Council.

Concurred in: PIG SMITH,
President of the Senate.

Approved: LEWIS DOWNING,
Principal Chief of the Cherokee Nation.

Tahlequah, C. N., November 18, 1868.

An Act Removing the Public School located at White Springs, near Lacy Hawkins', from said Springs to a point at or near the Mouth of Dog Creek, in Coo-wee-scoo-wee District.

Be it enacted by the National Council, That the Public School, now located at White Springs, on Grand River, near the residence of Lacy Hawkins, in Coo-wee-scoo-wee District, be, and the same (after the expiration of the present session) is hereby removed from said Springs, to a point at or near the mouth of Dog Creek, in said District.

PIG SMITH,
President of the Senate.

Concurred in: JOHN YOUNG,
Speaker of Council.

Approved: LEWIS DOWNING,
Principal Chief of the Cherokee Nation.

Tahlequah, C. N., November 20, 1868.

An Act Repealing An Act Authorizing Persons to Move into the Cherokee Nation, &c.

Be it enacted by the National Council, That the Act passed on the 15th of October, 1841, authorizing certain classes of persons to move into the Cherokee Nation without Memorializing the National Council, be, and the same is hereby Repealed.

JOHN YOUNG,
Speaker of Council.

Concurred in: PIG SMITH,
President of the Senate.

Approved: LEWIS DOWNING,
Principal Chief of the Cherokee Nation.

Tahlequah, C. N., November 20th, 1868.

An Act Authorizing the Publication of Penal Laws in the Manner Prescribed by the Treaty of 1866.

Whereas, It appears that an Act entitled, "An Act Regulating Trade," Approved November 7th, 1866; and an Act entitled, "An Act to Prohibit the Carrying of Weapons," Approved November 15th, 1866; (both of which are Penal Laws;) have not been Promulgated in the Manner Prescribed in the 7th Article of the Treaty of 1866, and are, in consequence, Inoperative as Laws: *Therefore,*

Be it enacted by the National Council, That the Principal Chief be, and he is hereby Requested and Authorized to have the Acts above-named Duly Promulgated in the manner indicated by the 7th Article of the Treaty of 1866, in such manner as, to him, seems the best calculated to have the Laws above-referred to, carried into effect at the earliest day practicable; and for this purpose he is hereby Authorized to Draw Warrants on the National Treasury to Defray the Expenses incurred in carrying this Act into Effect.

Be it futher enacted, That from and after the Passage of this Act, the Principal Chief shall be Required to cause the Publication of all Acts, "Prescribing a Penalty for their Violation" in One of the Two Ways Indicated by the 7th Article of the Treaty of 19th of July, 1866; as, to him, may seem best for the Public Interest, within Twenty Days after the close of the Session of the National Council passing the Act; and he shall enter a Certificate of such Publication, and the manner in which it was Published, on the Executive Register of Laws. And he is hereby Authorized to Draw Warrants on the National Treasury, Payable out of the General Fund, to defray the expenses of such Publication.

Be it further enacted, That it is hereby made the duty of the Sheriffs of the Respective Districts to Post all Penal Laws; Received from the Executive for that purpose; in a conspicuous manner at their respective Court-Houses, and to cause a Certificate of such Posting, and the Date thereof, to be placed in the hands of the Principal Chief, within Ten Days of such Posting; and that, where the Publication is done through Publication in a Newspaper, the Sheriff shall, in all cases, be required to Post the Act as if done in writing; and for this purpose the Principal Chief shall cause one or more copies of such Newspaper, as may print the Penal Law, to be furnished to each Sheriff in the Nation, at the cost of the Nation.

JOHN YOUNG,
Speaker of Council,

Concurred in:
PIG SMITH,
President of the Senate.

Presented and approved, 23d November, 1868.

LEWIS DOWNING,
Principal Chief of the Cherokee Nation.

Tahlequah, C. N. 14*th November*, 1868.

An Act re-admitting Messrs. John G. and Geo. W. Harnage, and their families, to Cherokee Citizenship.

Be it enacted by the National Council, That Messrs. John G. and Geo. W. Harnage, (Native-born Cherokees, that have been residing in Texas,) with their families, be, and they are hereby re-admitted to all the rights and privileges of native-born Cherokees.

PIG SMITH,
President of the Senate.

Concurred in: JOHN YOUNG,
Speaker of Council.

Approved: LEWIS DOWNING,
Principal Chief of the Cherokee Nation.

Tahlequah, C. N., Nov. 23, 1868.

An Act for the Prompt Payment of the Expenses of the Present Session of the National Council.

Be it enacted by the National Council, That the National Treasurer be authorized, and he is hereby required, to pay down in money, promptly, all warrants drawn upon him by the Principal Chief, for the payment of all expenses incurred at, and during the present regular term of the National Council, for the services of the various officers and members of the different Departments.

Be it further enacted, That the Principal Chief is hereby authorized and requested to issue promptly, at the close of the present term of the National Council, warrants for the payment of the said services, rendered in the different Departments during said term.

Approved: LEWIS DOWNING,
Principal Chief of the Cherokee Nation.

Tahlequah, C. N., Nov. 23, 1868.

An Act re-admitting William Harnage and Family to the Rights of Cherokee Citizenship.

Be it enacted by the National Council, That William

Harnage and family (Cherokees who have resided in the State of Texas) be, and they are hereby re-admitted to the rights of Cherokee Citizenship, according to the Laws and Constitution of the Cherokee Nation.

JOHN YOUNG,
Speaker of Council.

Concurred in: PIG SMITH,
President of the Senate.

Presented and approved, 24th November, 1868.

LEWIS DOWNING,
Principal Chief of the Cherokee Nation.

Tahlequah, C. N., Nov. 13, 1868.

An Act to Amend an Act entitled "An Act relative to the Court House in Coo-wee-scoo-wee District."

Be it enacted by the National Council, That the Act in relation to building a Court House in Coo-wee-scoo-wee District, passed December 7th, 1867, be so amended as to require the District Judge to have said Court House built at the Sulphur Springs, on the waters of Dog Creek, near Jesse Henry's, in said District, instead of the place designated in said Act, "Clermont's Mounds."

JOHN YOUNG,
Speaker of Council.

Concurred in: ELI SMITH,
President of Senate, pro tem.

Approved: LEWIS DOWNING,
Principal Chief of the Cherokee Nation.

Tahlequah, C. N., Nov. 23, 1868.

An Act for the Benefit of Cynthia Pack, and W. B. Taylor, and Lucy Man-Killer.

Be it enacted by the National Council, That the sum of One Hundred and Fifty Dollars, ($150.00), in favor of Cynthia Pack, due her for teaching a public school in

1862; and the sum of Thirty Dollars, ($30.00), Fifteen ($15.00) of which in favor of W. B. Taylor, and Fifteen Dollars ($15.00) in favor of Lucy Man-Killer, for taking care of two orphan children, while going to school in 1862, be, and the same is hereby appropriated, to be paid out of the fund provided for by the 23d Article of the Treaty of 1866, to meet the outstanding obligations of the Cherokee Nation; and the Principal Chief will be authorized to issue warrants accordingly.

ELI SMITH,
President of the Senate pro tem.

Concurred in: JOHN YOUNG,
Speaker of Council.

Approved: LEWIS DOWNING,
Principal Chief of the Cherokee Nation.

Tahlequah, C. N., Nov. 24, 1868.

An Act making an Appropriation in favor of Joseph Coody, and Spring Frog, Treasurer of the Cherokee Nation.

Be it enacted by the National Council, That the sum of Six Dollars ($6.00) in favor of Joseph Coody, and the sum of Seventeen Dollars and Fifty Cents (17.50) in favor of the Cherokee Nation, be, and the same are hereby appropriated, out of any funds in the Treasury not otherwise appropriated, belonging to the National Fund, to cover National Tickets to these amounts, issued by Joseph Coody, Acting Deputy Sheriff of Sequoyah District in 1867. The register of said Tickets has been lost or mislaid, so that the said Tickets have not been audited and registered according to law. And the Principal Chief will be authorized to issue warrants accordingly.

PIG SMITH,
President of the Senate.

Concurred in, with the following amendment: Add fifty cents to Joseph Coody's account, making $6.50 instead of $6.00.

JOHN YOUNG,
Speaker of Council.

Approved: LEWIS DOWNING,
Principal Chief of the Cherokee Nation.

Tahlequah, C. N., Nov. 23, 1868.

An Act for the Relief of Judge Elijah Butler.

Be it enacted by the National Council, That the sum of Fifty-One Dollars and Twenty-Five Cents be, and the same is hereby appropriated, out of any money in the National Treasury, belonging to the General Fund, not otherwise appropriated, for the use and benefit of Judge Elijah Butler, it being the amount due him for finishing of the Court House of Delaware District, in accordance with an Act of the National Council, of September, 1868. And the Principal Chief is hereby authorized to draw a warrant for the same.

ELI SMITH,
President of the Senate pro tem.

Concurred in: JOHN YOUNG,
Speaker of Council.

Approved: LEWIS DOWNING,
Principal Chief of the Cherokee Nation.

Tahlequah, C. N., Nov. 24, 1868.

An act Granting Cherokee Citizenship to W. S. Patton, and Robert B. Patton, Choctaws, that have inter-married among the Cherokees.

Be it enacted by the National Council, That William S. Patton and Robert B. Patton, Choctaws, that have intermarried among the Cherokees, be, and are hereby admitted to Cherokee Citizenship.

PIG SMITH,
President of the Senate.

Concurred in: JOHN YOUNG,
Speaker of Council.

Approved: LEWIS DOWNING,
Principal Chief of the Cherokee Nation.

Tahlequah, C. N., Nov. 25, 1868.

An Act to Protect the pbesent School House at Fort Gibson from the operation of the Act of 26th October, 1866, *entitled "An Act to Sell all Public Property at Fort Gibson."*

Be it enacted by the National Council, That the House

now used as a School House, in the Town of Fort Gibson, be, and it is hereby ordered to remain where it is, on the Public Square, for the period of One Year from the passage of this Act, if used in that time as a Public School House; and that it be, and it is hereby declared exempt from the operation of the Act of October 26th, 1866, entitled "An Act to Sell Public Property at Fort Gibson," during the same period; and from sale, by reason of its not having been removed, as the Act above referred to requires; all laws to the contrary notwithstanding.

PIG SMITH,
President of the Senate.

Concurred in: JOHN YOUNG,
Speaker of Council.

Approved: LEWIS DOWNING,
Principal Chief of the Cherokee Nation.

Tahlequah, C. N., Nov. 23, 1868.

An Act Providing for a National Printing Press.

Be it enacted by the National Council, That the Principal Chief be, and he is hereby authorized, as early as practicable, to designate some suitable person to purchase, in behalf of the Cherokee Nation, a Printing Press, with English and Cherokee types, and such material as is usually required in a printing establishment, for the ordinary purposes of newspaper, book, and job printing. *Provided*, That such purchase be made at a price not to exceed the sum of Three Thousand Dollars; for the payment of which the Principal Chief shall be authorized to issue warrants, to be paid out of any funds in the National Treasury, belonging to the National Fund, not otherwise appropriated.

Be it further enacted, That the Principal Chief shall be authorized to appoint a Superintendent, whose duty it shall be to take charge of the said Press, &c., and put the same in good condition for use; and to establish the same in the Supreme Court building, at Tahlequah, and to so manage and conduct it as not to interfere in any manner with the business of the Supreme Court, until otherwise provided by law.

Be it further enacted, That the Principal Chief be, and he is hereby, authorized to employ Two Competent Practical Printers, (one of whom shall be appointed Superintendent, as provided for above, and [who] shall be able to discharge his duties in both the Cherokee and English Languages). And the said Printers shall receive, as Compensation for their Services, such a reasonable allowance as may be agreed upon between them and the Principal Chief; payable Monthly, out of any Funds in the National Treasury, belonging to the National Fund, not Otherwise Appropriated; and the Principal Chief will be authorized to Draw Warrants accordingly.

Be it further enacted, That the said Superintendent, with his Assistant Printer, be, and they are hereby, required to do such Public Printing as may be required by the Principal Chief, in both the English and Cherokee Languages.

PIG SMITH,
President of the Senate.

Concurred in: JOHN YOUNG,
Speaker of Council.

Approved: LEWIS DOWNING,
Principal Chief of the Cherokee Nation.

Tahlequah, C. N., November 26th, 1868.

An Act to Amend An Act Entitled, "An Act to Organize the Nation into Eight Districts, and Establishing (Election) Precincts".

Be it enacted by the National Council, That the Act entitled, "An Act to Organize the Nation into Eight Districts, and Establishing Precincts of Election," Approved November 6th, 1840, be, and the same is hereby Amended as follows: That the Precinct of Election now established at a point at, or near, "Little John Rogers" (Se-quo-yah

District), be, and the same is hereby, Removed from said point to a point on Camp Creek, at the residence of Lewis Dayley, in said District.

PIG SMITH,
President of the Senate.

Concurred in:
JOHN YOUNG,
Speaker of Council.

Approved, 26th November, 1868:
LEWIS DOWNING,
Principal Chief of the Cherokee Nation.

Tahlequah, C. N., November 23d, 1868.

An Act Re-admitting Elijah Phillips to Citzenship.

Be it enacted by the National Council, That Elijah Phillips, formerly a citizen of the Cherokee Nation, be, and he is hereby, (together with his family), Re-admitted to all the Rights and Franchises of Cherokee Citizens.

PIG SMITH,
President of the Senate.

Concurred in:
JOHN YOUNG,
Speaker of Council.

Approved:
LEWIS DOWNING.
Principal Chief of the Cherokee Nation.

Tahlequah, C. N., November 26th, 1868.

Resolution to Adjourn.

Resolved by the National Council, That Tuesday next, the 1st day of December, 1868, be, and the same is fixed, as the day for the Adjournment of the Present Session of the National Council, at ten o'clock, A. M.

JOHN YOUNG,
Speaker of Council.

Concurred in:
PIG SMITH,
President of the Senate.

Approved:
LEWIS DOWNING,
Principal Chief of the Cherokee Nation.

Tahlequah, C. N., November 27th, 1868.

An Act for the Benefit of A. W. Timberlake.

Be it enacted by the National Council, That the Sum of Fourteen Dollars and Twenty-Five Cents be, and the same is hereby, appropriated out of any money belonging to the School Fund, not otherwise appropriated, for the Benefit of A. W. Timberlake; the same being [the] amount due him for Books furnished Baptist Mission School, by authority of the Superintendent of Public Schools.

PIG SMITH,
President of the Senate.

Concurred in: JOHN YOUNG,
Speaker of Council.

Approved: LEWIS DOWNING,
Principal Chief of the Cherokee Nation.

Tahlequah, C. N., November 28th, 1868.

An Act making an Appropriation for the Payment of "A List of Claims Registered for the Year 1868."

No.	Names.	Amount.
1	Johnson Foreman	$ 44 00
2	Fox Mouse	1 00
3	John Wickliffe	10 00
4	John Shell	2 00
5	W. G. Thornton	14 50
6	Jesse Wolf	4 00
7	William Snell	11 00
8	Flute Foxskin	2 00
9	John W. Stapler	138 88
10	R. A. Reese	8 00
11	John Rat	3 00
12	Moses (Sugar Mountain)	2 00
13	Ter-ni-no-lee	4 00
14	Arch Proctor	1 50
15	Joe Hawkins	4 00
16	Price Cochran	1 00
17	Mrs Fish	43 00

No.		Names.			Amount.
18	-	James Hendricks	-	-	$ 2 00
19	-	W. P. Ross	-	-	30 50
20	-	Taylor Sixkiller	-	-	5 00
21	-	Walter Christie	-	-	4 00
22	-	Allen Tanner	-	-	2 00
23	-	Ne-cow-ee	-	-	3 00
24	-	Frog Sixkiller	-	-	5 50
25	-	Elowee Butler	-	-	2 00
26	-	Joseph Coody	-	-	16 00
27	-	Joseph Shade	-	-	1 00
28	-	John Hunt	-	-	166 25
29	-	Josiah Vann	-	-	12 50
30	-	Soldier Sixkiller	-	-	3 00
31	-	F. H. Nash	-	-	375 25
32	-	James Bearpaw	-	-	2 00
33	-	Daniel Sixkiller	-	-	2 00
34	-	Charles Scraper	-	-	3 00
35	-	Cul-la-na-he-te	-	-	5 00
36	-	Archilla Foster	-	-	2 50
37	-	John C Cunningham	-	-	6 00
38	-	Levi Walkingstick	-	-	31 00
39	-	Richard Glory	-	-	3 00
40	-	Ca-taw-ka	-	-	2 50
41	-	Soldier Sixkiller	-	-	5 00
42	-	Albert Barnes	-	-	79 00
43	-	John T Adair	-	-	2 50
44	-	D H Ross & Bro's	-	-	11 75
45	-	Creek McCoy	-	-	45 00
46	-	John L Thompson	-	-	77 25
47	-	William Griffin	-	-	6 50
48	-	A W Timberlake	-	-	2 00
49	-	J A Johnson	-	-	52 00
50	-	Lewis Downing	-	-	900 00
51	-	James Vann	-	-	600 00
52	-	Spring Frog	-	-	603 10
53	-	David Rowe	-	-	300 00
54	-	Joseph Duval	-	-	300 00
55	-	Isaac Daniels	-	-	300 00

No.		Names.			Amount.
56	-	Daniel R Hicks	-	-	$192 75
57	-	Charles Wickliffe	-	-	200 00
58	-	Johnson Robbins	-	-	200 00
59	-	Jackson R Gourd	-	-	200 00
60	-	Samuel Adair	-	-	200 00
61	-	Franklin Falkner	-	-	76 00
62	-	Joseph Hilderbrand	-	-	200 00
63	-	Elowee Butler	-	-	200 00
64	-	Amos Thornton	-	-	200 00
65	-	D W Lipe	-	-	22 12
66	-	O P Brewer	-	-	60 00
67	-	George Benge	-	-	123 00
68	-	John Thornton	-	-	6 00
69	-	J W Adair	-	-	95 00
70	-	John L Springston	-	-	128 75
71	-	Moses Price	-	-	60 00
72	-	J L McCorkle	-	-	74 25
73	-	T J McGhee	-	-	68 25
74	-	Eli Spears	-	-	250 00
75	-	Jackson Christie	-	-	250 00
76	-	Ezekiel Proctor	-	-	250 00
77	-	William Snell	-	.	250 00
78	-	John G Schrimpsher	-	-	250 00
79	-	Bear Brown	-	-	253 75
80	-	Charles Drew	-	-	287 00
81	-	Jesse Baldridge	-	-	250 00
82	-	George Downing	-	-	250 00
83	-	John Lee	-	-	90 00
84	-	Jesse Redbird	-	-	150 00
85	-	Aaron Goingwolf	-	-	150 00
86	-	Levi Toney	-	-	150 00
87	-	Nelson Terrapin	-	-	150 00
88	-	John Kickup	-	-	137 50
89	-	Joseph Young	-	-	12 50
90	-	Moses Sixkiller	-	-	150 00
91	-	James Smith	-	-	150 00
92	-	John Grass	-	-	150 00
93	-	J F Thompson	-	-	110 50

No.		Names.	Amount.
94	-	Charlotte Benge - -	$ 94 00
95	-	Spencer S Stephens - -	30 00
96	-	Stand Grey - -	2 00
97	-	Jackson King - -	9 50
98	-	Joseph Swimmer - -	20 00
99	-	Joseph Coody - -	9 00
100	-	Adam Mouse - -	1 00
101	-	George Benge - -	7 00
102	-	John B Acorn - -	1 00
103	-	Runabout (Delaware District) -	2 00
104	-	Daniel (Delaware District) -	4 00
105	-	Aaron Tanner - -	2 00
106	-	Arch Vann - -	14 00
107	-	Sick-ee-tow-ee (Sequoyah District)	2 00
108	-	Coming (Tahlequah District) -	6 00
109	-	Middle Striker - -	8 00
110	-	Stephen Tehee - -	6 00
111	-	Wilson (Delaware District) -	2 00
112	-	Joseph Duval - -	12 40
113	-	John Rogers (Illinois District) -	1 00
114	-	Saunders Chote - -	2 00
115	-	George Blair - -	22 00
116	-	George W Scraper - -	5 00
117	-	John T Adair - -	105 00
118	-	J A Johnson - -	145 00
119	-	George W Scraper - -	130 00
120	-	W A Thompson - -	192 00
121	-	Jesse Feather - -	50 00
122	-	Eli Spears - -	50 00
123	-	John L Adair - -	3 50
124	-	Jackson Christie - -	7 50
125	-	Wah-la-nee-tah (Flint District) -	18 00
126	-	John Shell - -	1 00
127	-	Bear Brown - -	2 50
128	-	Susey Cooley - -	6 00
129	-	N B Saunders - -	
130	-	Jackson R Gourd - -	10 50
131	-	Mike Hilderbrand - -	2 00
132	-	Arch Scraper - -	2 00

No.		Names.			Amount.
133	-	Martha Parris	-	-	$ 3 00
134	-	C H Allen	-	-	3 00
135	-	Johnson Robbins	-	-	4 00
136	-	Arch Vann	-	-	2 00
137	-	Robin Smith	-	-	1 00
138	-	Joseph Seabolt	-	-	8 50
139	-	Keith (Flint District)	-	-	1 00
140	-	Oo squah loo car "	-	-	1 00
141	-	Jack Canoe	-	-	1 00
142	-	John Glass	-	-	1 00
143	-	Trotting Wolf	-	-	2 00
144	-	Sally Guess	-	-	300 00
145	-	Aaron Tanner	-	-	1 00
146	-	W A Daniel	-	-	2 00
147	-	Youngbird Muskrat	-	-	2 00
148	-	E B Saunders	-	-	2 00
149	-	Big Road	-	-	2 00
150	-	Chu war no ski (Delaware District)			1 00
151	-	Jumper (Going Snake District)		-	3 00
152	-	McCoy (Creek)	-	-	75 50
153	-	Stephen Foreman	-	-	6 00
154	-	Edmund Ross	-	-	12 00
155	-	Lewis A Ross	-	-	1 00
156	-	Charles R Gourd	-	-	38 00
157	-	C J Hanks	-	-	20 00
158	-	Stephen Tehee	-	-	26 00
159	-	George Whitmire	-	-	16 00
160	-	J L Thompson	-	-	2 25
161	-	T J McGhee	-	-	16 00
162	-	Um mu ar chu nu	-	-	1 00
163	-	O P Brewer	-	-	3 50
164	-	Ah nah tah wo he lor tah		-	20 00
165	-	Orrin Beck	-	-	20 00
166	-	Nancy Woodall	-	-	20 00
167	-	Lucy Downing	-	-	20 00
168	-	Goo die ee	-	-	20 00
169	-	Johnson Muskrat	-	-	20 00
170	-	Ahlee Osage	-	-	20 00
171	-	Che yun star	-	-	20 00

No.		Names.			Amount.
172	-	Joseph Drum	-	-	$ 20 00
173	-	Youngbird	-	-	20 00
174	-	Johnson Chu car la ti	-	-	20 00
175	-	Nancy Matoy	-	-	20 00
176	-	Peggy Quinton	-	-	20 00
177	-	Te sun too ski	-	-	20 00
178	-	Too nee	-	-	20 00
179	-	Wakee	-	-	20 00
180	-	Te car noo co wee ski	-	-	20 00
181	-	John Foreman	-	-	20 00
182	-	Sally Beehunter	-	-	20 00
183	-	Thomas John	-	-	20 00
184	-	Goose	-	-	20 00
185	-	Anne Glory	-	-	20 00
186	-	Claw sene	-	-	20 00
187	-	Daniel	-	-	20 00
188	-	Polly	-	-	20 00
189	-	Too cah	-	-	20 00
190	-	Rider Lizzard	-	-	20 00
191	-	Wah you lah	-	-	20 00
192	-	Betsey Backbone	-	-	20 00
193	-	Lizzy Terrell	-	-	20 00
194	-	Sa kee	-	-	20 00
195	-	Doublehead	-	-	20 00
196	-	Ailsey	-	-	20 00
197	-	A le tah (or Sow)	-	-	20 00
198	-	Lydia McPherson	-	-	20 00
199	-	Ezekiel Mankiller	-	-	20 00
200	-	Ni co chee	-	-	20 00
201	-	Major Bedstead	-	(Guardian)	20 00
202	-	Sale sey	-	"	20 00
203	-	John Lee	-	"	20 00
204	-	Crying Bear	-	"	20 00
205	-	Columbus Baldridge	-	"	20 00
206	-	Ah ne yar we ski	-	"	20 00
207	-	Esther Baldridge	-	"	20 00
208	-	George Blair	-	"	20 00
					$13,707 60

Be it enacted by the National Council, That the sum

of Thirteen Thousand, Seven Hundred and Seven Dollars, and Sixty Cents, be, and the same is hereby, appropriated, out of any money in the Treasury, not otherwise appropriated, belonging to the General Fund, for the use and benefit of the foregoing named persons, agreeable to the amounts set opposite each claimant's name; and the Principal Chief is hereby authorized to issue Warrants for the same.

CHARLES THOMPSON,
President of the Senate pro tem.

Concurred in: JOHN YOUNG,
Speaker of Council.

Approved: LEWIS DOWNING,
Principal Chief of the Cherokee Nation.

Tahlequah, C. N., November 28, 1868.

An Act Making an Appropriation to Defray the Expenses of the National Council, and to Pay the Claims of Members of the National Council, at the Annual Session [of] 1868.

No.	Names.	Amount.
1	Pig Smith	$128 00
2	Roach Young	136 00
3	Eli Smith	128 00
4	Fog	132 00
5	Alex Hawk	136 00
6	Charles Thompson	128 00
7	Frog Sixkiller	128 00
8	Cornsilk	128 00
9	Walter Christie	136 00
10	Oo-you-sut-tah	128 00
11	Joseph Coody	136 00
12	Mink Downing	136 00
13	James Mills	152 00
14	Robbin Smith	136 00
15	Allen Ross	147 00
16	Lewis A Ross	120 00
17	John Brewer	136 00

No.		Names.			Amount.
18	-	John P Davis	-	-	$136 00
19	-	Stephen Foreman	-	-	155 75
20	-	Black Fox	-	-	64 00
21	-	John Young	-	-	136 00
22	-	Joseph Cornsilk	-	-	128 00
23	-	John Rogers	-	-	132 00
24	-	George Drum	-	-	128 00
25	-	Sequoyah Tanner	-	-	128 00
26	-	Aaron Tanner	-	-	128 00
27	-	Daniel Muskrat	-	-	120 00
28	-	Writer	-	-	136 00
29	-	Jesse Thompson	-	-	128 00
30	-	John Glass	-	-	144 00
31	-	Stand Whirlwind	-	-	128 00
32	-	Ne-cow-ee Thompson	-	-	136 00
33	-	Daniel Redbird	-	-	128 00
34	-	Wilson Hair	-	-	128 00
35	-	Cho-ho-star	-	-	128 00
36	-	Tar-che-che	-	-	128 00
37	-	Nathaniel Fish	-	-	128 00
38	-	Stephen Teehee	-	-	136 00
39	-	Joseph Seabolt (corrected, $112 00)			136 00
40	-	Chi-chi	-	-	136 00
41	-	J C McCoy	-	-	136 00
42	-	C J Hanks	-	-	136 00
43	-	O P Brewer	-	-	136 00
44	-	Chicken Christie	-	-	128 00
45	-	Wah-la-nee-tah	-	-	128 00
46	-	Alex'r Scott	-	-	128 00
47	-	Arch Scraper	-	-	128 00
48	-	John Shell	-	-	128 00
49	-	Taylor Sixkiller	-	-	128 00
50	-	Thomas B Wolfe	-	-	150 00
51	-	Hog Carrier	-	-	64 00
52	-	J L Thompson	-	-	13 15
53	-	Moses Alberty	-	-	124 00
54	-	Jesse Henry	-	-	76 00
55	-	Samuel Smith	-	-	128 00

No.		Names.			Amount.
56	-	W L G Miller	-	-	$128 73
57	-	Big Arch	-	.	64 00
					$7,186 63
		Deduct error,	-	-	16 00
		Total,	-	-	$7,172 63
		Deduct error,	-	-	24 00
					$7,148 63

SCHOOL FUND.

Spencer S Stephens	-	-	$500 00
J L Thompson	-	-	100 70

Be it enacted by the National Council, That the sum of Seven Thousand, One Hundred and Seventy-Two Dollars, and Sixty-Three Cents, be, and the same is hereby, appropriated, out of [any money belonging to] the General Fund, not otherwise appropriated, for the use and benefit of the foregoing named persons, according to the amount set opposite each person's name; also, in accordance with an Act passed November 23d, 1868; and the Principal Chief is hereby authorized to draw Warrants for the same.

Be it further enacted, That the sum of Six Hundred Dollars and Seventy Cents be, and the same is hereby, appropriated, out of any money in the Treasury, belonging to the School Fund, not otherwise appropriated, for the use and benefit of Spencer S. Stephens and J. L. Thompson, according to the amounts set opposite each name; and the Principal Chief is hereby authorized to draw Warrants for the same.

PIG SMITH,
President of the Senate.

Concurred in, with the following Amendment:—Deduct Twenty-Four Dollars from Joseph Seabolt's account, for Six Days' [absence] error, leaving Seven Thousand, One Hundred and Forty-Eight Dollars and Sixty-Three Cents.

JOHN YOUNG,
Speaker of Council.

Concurred with the above Amendment.

PIG SMITH,
President of the Senate.

Approved: LEWIS DOWNING,
Principal Chief of the Cherokee Nation.

Tahlequah, C. N., Nov. 30, 1868.

An Act Making an Appropriation "for the Services of Clerks, &c.," for the Year 1868.

No.	Names.	Amount.
1	Charles Rogers	$ 60 00
2	J B Mayes	60 00
3	Jesse Shell	2 00
4	George W Ross	60 00
5	Henry Scraper	26 00
6	Big Arch	4 00
7	Logan Duval	50 00
8	Joseph Duval	45 00
9	F H Nash	92 00
10	William Mills	15 00
11	Mrs Smith Christie	100 00
12	Chi-chi	36 00
13	James Swimmer	48 00
14	Arch Scraper	143 00
15	Aaron Tanner	150 00
16	Wat Christie and Jesse Henry	1,915 00
17	Alex'r Hawk	100 00
18	Daniel Muskrat	50 00
19	Charles Pettit	100 00
20	Rider Rattling Gourd	50 00
21	Isaac Turner	50 00
22	Thomas Pott	115 00
23	James Tincup	50 00
24	Lewis Downing	365 00
25	Lewis Downing	100 00
26	Chi-chi	30 00
27	Writer	61 00

No.		Names.			Amount.
28	-	Keith	-	-	6 00
29	-	Glass	-	-	30 00
30	-	Stand Whirlwind	-	-	50 00
31	-	Alex'r Scott	-	-	35 00
32	-	Taylor Sixkiller	-	-	50 00
33	-	Cornsilk (Illinois)	-	-	35 09
34	-	Arch Scraper	-	-	120 00
35	-	Arch Keener	-	-	16 00
36	-	N Thompson	-	-	26 00
37	-	Charles R Gourd	-	-	75 00
38	-	Mrs Martha Aaron	-	-	20 00
39	-	Rider Swimmer	-	-	40 00
40	-	Margaret Sourjohn	-	-	15 00
41	-	Hunter Brown	-	-	35 00
42	-	Frog Sixkiller	-	-	60 00
43	-	Nathaniel Fish	-	-	40 00
44	-	Nathaniel Fish	-	-	10 00
45	-	John Hicks	-	-	50 00
46	-	John Hicks	-	-	20 00
47	-	Frog Sixkiller	-	-	12 00
48	-	Jane Sixkiller	-	-	35 00
49	-	George Scraper	-	-	188 00
50	-	Redbird Sixkiller	-	-	44 00
51	-	W L G Miller	-	-	156 17
52	-	Alex'r Vann	-	-	1 00
53	-	Cloud Tickstring	-	-	20 00
54	-	Mary Ann Bean	-	-	20 00
55	-	Lesse (Flint District)	-	-	20 00
56	-	Samuel Downing	-	-	16 00
57	-	J B Jones	-	-	16 00
58	-	George W Ross	-	-	5 75
59	-	Jesse Wolfe	-	-	31 00
					$5,174 92

SCHOOL FUND.

Stephen Foreman	-	-	60 00
J L Thompson	-	-	65 00
W P Boudinot	-	-	60 00
			$ 185 00

ORPHAN FUND.

John Alberty	-	-	30 00
Luther Crutchfield	-	-	45 00
			$ 75 00

Be it enacted by the National Council, That the sum of Five Thousand One Hundred and Seventy-Four Dollars and Ninety-Two Cents, be, and the same is hereby, appropriated, out of the General Fund, not otherwise appropriated, for the use and benefit of the foregoing named persons, according to the amount set opposite each person's name; and the Principal [Chief] is hereby authorized to draw Warrants for the same.

Be it further enacted, That the sum of One Hundred and Eighty-Five Dollars be, and the same is hereby, appropriated, out of the School Fund, not otherwise appropriated, for the use and benefit of Stephen Foreman, J. L. Thompson, and W. P. Boudinot, according to the amounts set opposite each name; and the Principal Chief is hereby authorized to draw Warrants for the same.

Be it further enacted, That the sum of Seventy-Five Dollars be, and the same is hereby, appropriated, out of the Orphan Fund, not otherwise appropriated, for the use and benefit of John Alberty and Luther Crutchfield, according to the amounts set opposite each name; and the Principal Chief is hereby authorized to draw Warrants for the same.

PIG SMITH,
President of the Senate.

Concurred in: JOHN YOUNG,
Speaker of Council.

Approved: LEWIS DOWNING,
Principal Chief of the Cherokee Nation.

Tahlequah, C. N., December 1*st*, 1868.

An Act making an Appropriaton for the Support of the Public Schools, for the year 1869, *the Maintenance of Orphans, and the Purchase of Books and Stationery.*

Be it enacted by the National Council, That the sum

of Eight Thousand Dollars ($8,000.00) be, and the same is hereby, appropriated, out of any money in the National Treasury, belonging to the School Fund, not otherwise appropriated, for the support of the several Public Schools, during the ensuing year, 1869.

Be it further enacted, That the sum of Two Thousand and Seven Hundred Dollars ($2,700.00) be, and the same is hereby, appropriated, out of any money in the National Treasury, belonging to the Orphan Fund, for the clothing and board of the several Orphan Children who may be attending the Public Schools, as Scholars, during the ensuing year of 1869.

Be it further enacted, That the sum of Two Hundred Dollars ($200.00) be, and the same is hereby, appropriated, out of any money in the National Treasury, not otherwise appropriated, belonging to the School Fund, for the purchase of Books and Stationery, for the use of the Public Schools, for the ensuing year; and the Principal Chief is hereby authorized to draw a warrant in favor of Spencer S. Stephens, for the same.

PIG SMITH,
President of the Senate.

Concurred in: JOHN YOUNG,
Speaker of Council.

Approved: LEWIS DOWNING,
Principal Chief of the Cherokee Nation.

Tahlequah, C. N., December 1, 1868.

An Act making an Appropriation for the Benefit of T. B. Wolfe, and Company, &c.

Be it enacted by the National Council, That the sum of Five Hundred and Sixty-Three Dollars and Fifty Cents, ($563.50), be, and the same is hereby appropriated, out of any money in the Treasury, belonging to the General Fund, not otherwise appropriated, for the use of T. B. Wolfe and Company; also, Twenty-five Dollars, to T. B. Wolfe; and the Principal Chief is authorized to issue warrants for the same.

PIG SMITH,
President of the Senate.

Concurred in: JOHN YOUNG,
Speaker of Council.

Approved: LEWIS DOWNING,
Principal Chief of the Cherokee Nation.

Tahlequah, C. N., December 1, 1868.

LAWS

ENACTED AND

JOINT RESOLUTIONS

PASSED BY THE NATIONAL COUNCIL

OF THE

CHEROKEE NATION;

DURING AN EXTRA SESSION,

CONVENED BY THE PRINCIPAL CHIEF,

ON THE 21ST OF SEPTEMBER, 1868.

Resolution of the National Council, Requiring Principal Chief to Furnish it with Compiled Laws.

Resolved by the National Council, That the Principal [Chief] be, and he is hereby, requested and authorized to furnish the Senate and Council, each, with two copies of the Compiled Laws, for the use and benefit of the National Council; also, one copy, each, of the Treaty of 1866.

ARCH. SCRAPER,
Speaker of the Council pro tem.

Concurred in, by adding the word "Chief" to the above resolution.

PIG SMITH,
President of the Senate.

Approved: LEWIS DOWNING,
Principal Chief of the Cherokee Nation.

Tahlequah, C. N., September 23, 1868.

An Act Authorizing the Prompt Payment of the Expenses of the Extra Session of the National Council, Convened 21st September, 1868.

Be it enacted by the National Council, That the Treasurer of the Cherokee Nation be, and he is hereby, authorized and required to pay all expenses of the Extra Session of the National Council, (convened on Monday, the 21st instant), out of any money now in the National Treasury, belonging to the National or General Fund; and the Principal Chief is hereby authorized to draw warrants accordingly.

PIG SMITH,
President of the Senate.

Concurred in: ARCH. SCRAPER,
Speaker of Council pro tem.

Approved: LEWIS DOWNING,
Principal Chief of the Cherokee Nation.

Tahlequah, C. N., September 24, 1868.

Resolution of the National Council, Authorizing the Principal Chief to Furnish Superintendent of Indian Affairs, and the Cherokee Agent, with a Copy, each, of the Compiled Laws.

Resolved, by the National Council, That the Principal Chief be, and he is hereby, authorized to furnish the Hon. Superintendent of Indian Affairs, and [the] Cherokee Agent, each, with a copy of the Compiled Laws of the Cherokee Nation.

ARCH. SCRAPER,
Speaker of Council pro tem.

Concurred in: PIG SMITH,
President of the Senate.

Approved: LEWIS DOWNING,
Principal Chief of the Cherokee Nation.

Tahlequah, C. N., September 24, 1868.

Resolution of the National Council, Granting Use of the Male Seminary to the Superintendent of Indian Affairs, for the Purposes Therein Named.

Resolved by the National Council, That L. N. Robinson, Superintendent of Indian Affairs, Southern Superintendency, be permitted to occupy the Male Seminary, for the purpose of holding the "Grand Council;" and for use as Head Quarters of Superintendent of Indian Affairs, Southern Superintendency, for one year, unless said building should sooner be wanted for School purposes.

PIG SMITH,
President of the Senate.

Concurred in:
ARCH. SCRAPER,
Speaker of Council pro tem.

Approved:
LEWIS DOWNING,
Principal Chief of the Cherokee Nation.

Tahlequah, C. N., September 25, 1868.

An Act to Re-Appoint a Delegation.

WHEREAS, It is recommended by the Principal Chief, in his Message of the 22d instant, that the late Delegation to Washington be re-appointed; therefore,

Be it enacted by the National Council, That John P. Davis, H. D. Reese, Arch. Scraper, W. P. Adair, and Samuel Smith, be, and they are hereby, re-appointed a Delegation to visit Washington City, accompanied by the Principal Chief.

PIG SMITH,
President of Senate.

Concurred in:
ARCH. SCRAPER,
Speaker of Council pro tem.

Approved:
LEWIS DOWNING.
Principal Chief of the Cherokee Nation.

Tahlequah, C. N., September 28th, 1868.

An Act in relation to the Election of Members of the Grand Council.

WHEREAS, By the 12th Article of the Treaty of 1866,

between the United States and the Cherokee Nation, it is agreed by the Cherokees that a General Council, consisting of Delegates elected by each Nation, or Tribe, lawfully within the Indian Territory, may be annually convened in said Territory, which Council shall be organized in such manner, and with such powers, as are in said Treaty prescribed; and

WHEREAS, The proper authority has prescribed the time and place for the meeting of said General Council, and fixed the number of Delegates, to be chosen by the Cherokees; therefore,

Be it enacted by the National Council, That the Principal Chief be, and he is hereby, authorized to issue his Proclamation, ordering an Election to be held at the several Precincts of the Cherokee Nation, established by law, on Wednesday, the 28th day of October, 1868, for the election of Sixteen Delegates, to represent the Cherokee Nation, at the said General Council, to be divided and apportioned as follows, to-wit:—Two for Canadian District; One for Sequoyah District; One for Flint; Two for Going Snake; One for Delaware; Three for Coo-wee-scoo-wee, including one Delaware; Two for Tahlequah; Two for Saline; and Two for Illinois [Districts]; to be chosen by a majority of the voters of said Districts; and said Election shall be held and conducted, in all respects, as the Constitution and Laws of the Cherokee Nation provide, for the election of Principal and Assistant Principal Chiefs, and the Returns thereof shall be made to the President of the National Senate, on or before the Second Monday in November, 1868, and by whom, in presence of both Houses of the National Council, they shall be opened; and the persons having the highest number of votes in said District shall be declared to be elected as said Delegates, and shall be duly commissioned as such, by the Principal Chief.

Be it further enacted, That said Delegates shall hold their office until the next General Election, in August,

1869, when there shall be another election held in like manner, unless otherwise ordered by law.

PIG SMITH,
President of Senate.

Concurred in: ARCH. SCRAPER,
Speaker of Council pro tem.

Approved: LEWIS DOWNING,
Principal Chief of the Cherokee Nation.

Tahlequah, C. N., September 28, 1868.

An Act Designating the Place of Holding Courts in Delaware District.

Be it enacted by the National Council, That the place of holding Courts in Delaware District shall be at William Tucker's Prairie, in said District.

Be it further enacted, That the District Judge of said District is hereby authorized to have the unfinished building completed, (that was raised for the Court House), and report the amount of expenses to the National Council for settlement.

PIG SMITH,
President of the Senate.

Concurred in: ARCH. SCRAPER,
Speaker of Council pro tem.

Approved: LEWIS DOWNING,
Principal Chief of the Cherokee Nation.

Tahlequah, C. N., September 29, 1868.

An Act to Re-Establish Two Election Precincts in Coo-wee-scoo-wee District.

WHEREAS, Two Precincts in Coo-wee-scoo-wee District, to-wit:—At Richard Coody's old place, and Caney Precinct, at or near James Peak's, have been abandoned for the two previous Elections; therefore,

*Be it enacted by the National Connci*l, That the above named Precincts be, and they are hereby, re-established, and that the Judge of the District Court appoint Judges and Clerks accordingly.

JOHN YOUNG,
Speaker of Council.

Concurred in: PIG SMITH,
President of the Senate..

Approved: LEWIS DOWNING,
Principal Chief of the Cherokee Nation.

Tahlequah, C. N. September 30, 1868.

An Act to amend an Act, passed December 9*th*, 1867, *for Buildinj a Capitol for the use of the National Council, &c., &c., in the Town of Tahlequah.*

Be it enacted by the National Council, That the Act passed December 9, 1867, in regard to [the] building the Capitol, be amended, so that the "Goodlander" plan of the Building be adopted, instead of the present plan of the Building.

Be it further enacted, That the Contractors for said Building be allowed until the 1st day of October, 1869, to complete said Building.

Be it further enacted, That the additional sum of Seven Thousand Dollars, or so much thereof as will be necessary, be appropriated out of any money in the Treasury, belonging to the General Fund, not otherwise appropriated, to defray the expenses of building said Capitol. And the Principal Chief is hereby authorized to draw a warrant for the same.

PIG SMITH,
President of the Senate.

Concurred in: JOHN YOUNG,
Speaker of Council.

Approved: LEWIS DOWNING,
Principal Chief of the Cherokee Nation.

Tahlequah, C. N., September 30, 1868.

Resolution Setting the Time for Adjournment of National Council.

Be it Resolved by the National Council, That the National Council adjourn on Friday Morning, at 10 o'clock, the 2nd day of October, 1868.

PIG SMITH,
President of the Senate.

Concurred in: JOHN YOUNG,
Speaker of Council.

Approved: LEWIS DOWNING,
Principal Chief of the Cherokee Nation.

Tahlequah, C. N., September 30, 1868.

An Act to Instruct the Cherokee Delegation.

WHEREAS, A Delegation representing the full interests of the Cherokee Nation, and People, before the Government of the United States, under an Act of the National Council, of December 11th, 1867, have recently visited the City of Washington, in the performance of the duties of their mission, and have reported accordingly; and

WHEREAS, The duties of the said Delegation are still unfinished; and the National Council have authorized Lewis Downing, Principal Chief, H. D. Reese, Samuel Smith, Arch. Scraper, J. P. Davis, and W. P. Adair, of said Delegation, to return to the City of Washington, and to bring to a satisfactory adjustment and conclusion the interests of the Cherokee Nation and People, still unfinished by them; therefore,

Be it enacted by the National Council, That the said Delegation be, and they are hereby, instructed to carry out the instructions of the said Act of the National Council of December 11th, 1867, at their earliest opportunity, and to make their report accordingly, as soon after the object of their mission shall have been completed as is practicable.

Be it further enacted, That the Delegation is hereby further instructed, to protest against the claim of the North Carolina Cherokees, for an equal proportion, according to numbers, of the Lands, Annuities, and other Moneys, belonging to the Cherokee Nation.

Approved: LEWIS DOWNING,
Principal Chief of the Cherokee Nation.
Tahlequah, C. N., October 1, 1868.

An Act Making an Appropriation for the Payment of Claims of Members of the National Council, and [of] the Executive Council, for Services [during] Extra Session of National Council, September 21, 1868.

No.	Names.	Amount.
1	Allen Ross	$ 50 00
2	Lewis A Ross	48 00
3	John P Davis	64 00
4	John Brewer	64 00
5	Joseph Coody	66 00
6	Mink Downing	64 00
7	Frog Sixkiller	56 00
8	Cornsilk	56 00
9	Alex'r Hawk	64 00
10	Oo-you-sut-tah	56 00
11	Walter Christie	56 00
12	Eli Smith	56 00
13	Fog	28 00
14	Robert Smith	64 00
15	James Mills	48 00
16	Pig Smith	56 00
17	Roach Young	56 00
18	Stephen Foreman	72 85
19	Black Fox	28 00
20	John Young	28 00
21	John Rogers	64 00
22	Chicken Christie	56 00
23	Wilson Hair	56 00
24	Sequoyah Tanner	64 00
25	Aaron Tanner	64 00
26	Joseph Cornsilk	56 00

No.		Names.			Amount.
27	-	Stand Whirlwind	-	-	56 00
28	-	Daniel Redbird	-	-	56 00
29	-	Arch Scraper	-	-	56 00
30	-	Jesse Thompson	-	-	72 00
31	-	Writer	-	-	64 00
32	-	John Glass	-	-	60 00
33	-	Joseph Seabolt	-	-	64 00
34	-	Stephen Teehee	-	-	64 00
35	-	C J Hanks	-	-	64 00
36	-	John Shell	-	-	56 00
37	-	Taylor Sixkiller	-	-	56 00
38	-	Che-che	-	-	64 00
39	-	J C McCoy	-	-	64 00
40	-	Daniel Muskrat	-	-	64 00
41	-	Cho-ho-stah	-	-	52 00
42	-	Wah-la-nee-tah	-	-	56 00
43	-	Alex'r Scott	-	-	56 00
44	-	Ne-cow-ee Thompson	-	-	56 00
45	-	Tah-che-che	-	-	56 00
46	-	N Fish	-	-	48 00
47	-	O P Brewer	-	-	64 00
48	-	George Drum	-	-	56 00
49	-	T B Wolfe	-	-	65 60
50	-	Hog Carrier	-	-	28 00
51	-	Samuel Smith	-	-	56 00
52	-	Moses Alberty	-	-	56 00
53	-	W L G Miller	-	-	57 95
54	-	Archy	-	-	28 00
					$3,034 40

Be it enacted by the National Council, That the sum of Three Thousand and Thirty-Four Dollars and Forty Cents be, and the same is hereby, appropriated, out of any money in the Treasury, belonging to the General Fund, not otherwise appropriated, for the use and benefit of the foregoing named persons, according to the amounts set opposite each person's name, and in accordance with an Act passed

24th of September, 1868; and the Principal Chief is hereby authorized to draw Warrants for the same.

Approved: LEWIS DOWNING,

Principal Chief of the Cherokee Nation.

Tahlequah, C. N., October 1st, 1868.

ACTS OF THE NATIONAL COUNCIL,

AND

JOINT RESOLUTIONS,

MADE AND ADOPTED

AT THE REGULAR SESSION

OF NOVEMBER, 1869.

An Act Requiring the Auditor of Accounts to Remain at the Seat of Government, to Perform such Duties as may be Assigned him by the Senate, During the Present Session of the National Council; and Allowing him a Per Diem, in Addition to his Salary, for such Services.

WHEREAS, W. P. Mackey, Auditor of Accounts, is still engaged in Registering Claims, and discharging all the duties of Auditor of Accounts, and board being high—therefore,

Be it enacted by the National Council, That W. P. Mackey, Auditor of Accounts, be, and he is hereby, required to remain at the Seat of Government, during the present Session of the National Council, to perform such duties as registering Claims, and preparing Appropriation Bills, and such other duties as the Senate may require of him.

Be it further enacted, That the Auditor of Accounts be,

and he is hereby, allowed a compensation of Four Dollars per day additional to his salary, during actual service.

Approved: LEWIS DOWNING,
Principal Chief of the Cherokee Nation.
Tahlequah, C. N., Nov. 18, 1869.

An Act to Adopt I. N. Parker, a Seneca Indian, a Member of the Cherokee Nation.

Be it enacted by the National Council, That I. Newton Parker, a member of the Tonawanda Band of the Seneca Indians, resident within the limits of the State of New York, be, and he is hereby, Adopted as a Member of the Cherokee Nation, and admitted to all the Rights, Privileges, and Immunities of a Native-born Citizen of said Nation.

Approved: LEWIS DOWNING,
Principal Chief of the Cherokee Nation.
Tahlequah, C. N., November 17, 1869.

An Act to Provide for Compiling, Translating, and Printing certain Books in the Cherokee Language.

Be it enacted by the National Council, That Rev. John B. Jones, Rev. Stephen Foreman, and Wm. P. Boudinot, be, and they are hereby, constituted a Committee, for the purpose of selecting an Elementary Arithmetic, an Elementary Geography, and a small Compilation of History, to be Translated, and Printed in the Cherokee Language, in such form as may be best adapted to impart a knowledge of the same, and to aid those who do not speak the English Language, to acquire a knowledge of that Language.

Be it further enacted, That Rev. John B. Jones be authorized to Translate said Books into the Cherokee Language; and the Principal Chief to cause the same to be Printed at the National Printing Office, or wherever the same can be done in the most economical manner; and the person authorized to Translate the Books provided for by this Act, shall be allowed Three Dollars per day while so engaged.

Approved: LEWIS DOWNING,

Principal Chief of the Cherokee Nation.

Tahlequah, C. N., November 23, 1869.

An Act to Establish a National Newspaper.

Be it enacted by the National Council, That there shall be established, in Tahlequah, a National Newspaper, of medium size, to be called "The Cherokee Advocate;" and which shall have for its objects, the diffusion of important information among the Cherokee People, the advancement of the general interests of the Cherokee Nation, and other Indian Tribes, and the defence of Indian Rights; and which shall be published Weekly, in the English and Cherokee Languages. *Provided,* Nothing of a partizan character, in regard to persons or politics in the Cherokee Nation, shall be admitted into the columns of said Paper.

Be it further enacted, That there shall be elected, by the National Council, for the term of Two Years, an Editor, who shall exercise control over the whole establishment, receive all subscription money, and account quarterly to the National Treasurer for the same; and make annually, to the National Council, a full report of the condition of the Paper, and its interests; and who shall receive, as his salary, the sum of Seven Hundred Dollars per annum. The Brick Court House, in Tahlequah, is also placed in his charge, for use as a Printing Office; and said Editor shall be authorized to have such alterations made of the interior as will best fit the building for such purpose. Said Editor shall be also authorized, from time to time, to purchase and obtain such necessary material, and provide for the transportation thereof, as may be required for the Publishing of such Newspaper, and for such other Printing as may be required by the National Council.

In further pursuance of his duties, said Editor shall be authorized to employ, upon reasonable terms, such labor as may be absolutely required to do the work of the Office. *Provided,* That any contract made with Printers, under authority of this Act, shall first be approved by the Principal Chief.

That the Principal Chief be, and he is hereby, authorized to appoint a suitable person, whose duty it shall be to Translate into the Cherokee Language, for publication, such Laws, Public Documents, and other articles, as the Editor may submit to him for that purpose, and whose salary shall be Five Hundred Dollars per annum; and the pay of Printers to be paid Quarterly, upon the Warrants of the Principal Chief, to be drawn upon the General Fund, who is hereby authorized to draw the same accordingly.

The Editor shall be subject to removal by the Principal Chief, for failure to perform the duties of his office; in which event the Principal Chief shall be authorized to fill the vacancy by appointment, until the next meeting of the Council.

Be it further enacted, That the sum of Five Hundred Dollars, or so much of it as may be necessary, is hereby appropriated, out of any money in the Treasury, belonging to the General Fund, to defray the expenses of preparing the Office, and commencing the Publication of said Newspaper; and the Principal Chief is authorized to draw Warrants accordingly, upon being presented with Exhibits of such expense, certified to by the Editor.

Be it further enacted, That the Terms of Subscription for said Paper shall be Two Dollars per Annum, in Money, National Warrants, or Certificates. The Rates of Advertising shall be fixed by the Editor, except such Advertisements as may be required of Public Officers, by Law, which shall be inserted without charge. And at the commencement of each Session of Council, the Editor shall report the amount received, and all other matters of interest connected with the Office, through the Principal Chief, to the National Council.

Be it further enacted, That the Editor, Translator, and Printer of said Paper, be, and they are hereby, required to give Bond and Security to the Treasurer of the Nation, for the faithful discharge of their duties, in a sum double the amount of their respective salaries.

Approved: LEWIS DOWNING,
Principal Chief of the Cherokee Nation.
Tahlequah, C. N., November 23d, 1869.

An Act to Amend the "Act to Regulate the Issue of Pensions."

Be it enacted by the National Council, That the Act passed December 16, 1867, be, and the same is hereby, so amended, that it shall be the duty of the Judge of the District Court, wherein an applicant is resident, to take testimony in all cases of Pensions already granted, and in all cases of application for Pensions hereafter, which testimony must be based on the circumstances embraced in the said Act. The affidavit must be supported by the testimony of at least two witnesses, to be taken down in writing, by the Judge of the District Court, where such application is made, and the same furnished to the Principal Chief, to be laid before the National Council, for their action, and the appropriation made according to the nature and condition of the applicant.

Be it further enacted, That the Judge of the District Court, where such applicant may reside, shall appoint some suitable and responsible person Guardian for such Pensioners, who shall present a certificate of appointment, from the Judge of the District Court, to the Auditor of Public Accounts, to be registered, with the name of the Pensioner, and the amount of Pension allowed him by law; the amount to be paid to the Guardian of said Pensioner.

Approved: LEWIS DOWNING,
Principal Chief of the Cherokee Nation.
Tahlequah, C. N., November 23, 1869.

An Act to Amend "An Act in Relation to Tax on Stock Passing Through and Grazing in the Cherokee Nation."

Be it enacted by the National Council, That in all cases where any one of the Sheriffs of the several Districts may have reason to believe that efforts are being made to evade the Law, requiring the payment of a Tax for Stock passing through or grazing in the Cherokee Nation, by collusion of any citizen or citizens claiming such Stock, that such Sheriff shall be authorized, and it is hereby made his duty, to put such citizen or citizens, so claiming, on oath, and question them, as to the *bona fide* owner of such Stock, so claimed; and in all such cases, if it be ascertained that there is an existing understanding between the owner of any such Stock, and any citizen, or citizens, for the purpose of evading the Law requiring the payment of a Tax on Stock, passing through or grazing in the Cherokee Nation, then, in that case, it shall be the duty of such Sheriff to collect double the amount of Tax which would otherwise have been due under the said Law—one-half for the benefit of the National Treasury, and one-half for the Sheriff making such collection.

Be it further enacted, That in case such citizen, or citizens, shall refuse to answer, on oath, as above provided, such questions as the Sheriff may ask, in relation to the ownership of such Stock, then it shall be the duty of such Sheriff to report the facts to the Solicitor of the District, and to assist the Solicitor in the prosecution of such citizen, or citizens, of the Cherokee Nation, as may be guilty of a refusal to answer, on his or their oath, as herein-before provided for, thereby violating, and aiding and abetting in the violation, by others, of the Revenue or Tax Laws of the Cherokee Nation. And, upon conviction, such citizen, or citizens, so refusing to answer, shall be fined in a sum not less than One Hundred Dollars, nor more than Seven Hundred Dollars—one-half of said Fine to belong equally to the Sheriff and Solicitor so prosecuting, and the other half for the benefit of the National Treasury. And the term: "Driving Stock through this Nation," in said Act of 16th December, 1867, shall be taken and held to be travelling through the country at a rate, on a direct travelled route, towards point of destination, of not less than fifteen miles per day, with Mules and Horses; ten miles, with Cattle; and five miles, with Sheep, Hogs and Goats. *Provided*, That unavoidable detention by high water shall not be construed as a violation of this provision.

Approved: LEWIS DOWNING,

Principal Chief of the Cherokee Nation.

Tahlequah, C. N., November 25, 1869.

An Act for Repairing Canadian Court House.

Be it enacted by the National Council, That the District Judge in Canadian District be, and he is hereby, authorized and directed to appoint a Committee, and to employ some one, under written contract, to repair the Court House in Canadian District. *Provided*, The expense of said repairs shall not exceed Two Hundred Dollars.

Approved: LEWIS DOWNING,

Principal Chief of the Cherokee Nation.

Tahlequah, C. N., November 26th, 1869.

An Act Making an Appropriation to Complete the Court House in Flint District.

Be it enacted by the National Council, That the sum of One Hundred Dollars be, and the same is hereby, appropriated, out of any money in the Treasury, belonging to the General Fund, not otherwise appropriated, to complete the Court House in Flint District; and the Principal Chief is hereby authorized to draw a Warrant in favor of District Judge for the same.

Approved: LEWIS DOWNING.

Principal Chief of the Cherokee Nation.

Tahlequah, C. N., November 25th, 1869.

An Act Appropriating Four Hundred and Nine Dollars and Seventy-Six Cents, for Special Purposes, out of the School Fund.

Be it enacted by the National Council, That the sum of Four Hundred and Nine Dollars and Seventy-Six Cents be, and the same is hereby, appropriated, out of any money belonging to the School Fund, not otherwise appropriated, for the following named persons; and the Principal Chief is authorized to draw Warrants accordingly:

For J. P. Lippincott,	- - -	$ 85 00
" F. H. Nash,	- - -	53 94
" J. M. Bryan & Co.,	- - -	32 72
" J. W. Stapler,	- - -	215 70
" W. H. Rhea,	- - -	14 40
" E. J. Parks,	- - -	8 00
		$409 76

Approved: LEWIS DOWNING,
Principal Chief of the Cherokee Nation.
Tahlequah, C. N., November 29, 1869.

An Act Making Appropriations for the Support of the Public Schools, &c., for the Year 1869–'70.

SECTION 1. *Be it enacted by the National Council*, That the sum of Fourteen Thousand Eight Hundred Dollars be, and the same is hereby, appropriated, out of any money in the Treasury, belonging to the School Fund, not otherwise appropriated, for the pay of Teachers of the Public Schools, for the year 1869–70. Also, the sum of Six Hundred Dollars, or so much thereof as may be necessary, for the purchase of Books and Stationery, for the use of the Public Schools, to be expended under the direction of the Superintendent of Schools. Also, the sum of Five Hundred Dollars, to defray the Salary of the Superintendent of Public Schools, for the year 1869–70, and to be paid to him in semi-annual installments. Also, the sum of Nine Hundred Dollars, to pay, for the year 1869–70, one Assistant Teacher for the Public School at Tahlequah, one for the School at Fort Gibson, and one for the School at Baptist Mission, in Going Snake District. Also, the sum of One Hundred and Seventy-Five Dollars, or Five Dollars per School, to be paid to the Directors of the Schools, for expenses incurred by them, in necessary repair of School Houses.

Sec. 2. *Be it further enacted*, That the sum of Four Thousand Three Hundred and Twenty Dollars be, and it is hereby, appropriated, out of any money in the Treasury, belonging to the Orphan Fund, not otherwise appropriated, for the board and clothing of Orphan Children, attending the Public Schools, during the year 1869–70, at the rate of four Orphans per School.

Sec. 3. *Be it further enacted*, That the Superintendent of Schools is hereby authorized to remove the Public School from the Moravian Mission, and locate the same at Oak Grove, in Going Snake District; and also, to establish one new School at Viann Camp Ground, near Joseph Duval's, and one Colored School at Fort Gibson, in Illinois District; also, one School at Capt. Fish's, in Tahlequah District; one near Contention Spring, in Delaware District; one near Ellis Saunders', in Sequoyah District; and one near Delaware Miller's, in Coo-wee-scoo-wee District. And the Principal Chief is hereby authorized to draw Warrants on the Treasury for the sums herein above appropriated, in accordance with the provisions of existing laws relating thereto.

ARCH. SCRAPER,
President of Senate.

Geo. W. Johnson,
Clerk of Senate.

Concurred in, with the following Amendment:—In Sec. 2, and last line, strike out the words: "*at the rate of four Orphans per School.*"

STAND WHIRLWIND,
Speaker of Council.

T. B. Wolfe,
Clerk of Council.

Amendment concurred in:

ARCH. SCRAPER,
President of Senate.

Geo. W. Johnson,
Clerk of Senate.

Approved: LEWIS DOWNING,
Principal Chief of the Cherokee Nation.

Tahlequah, C. N., November 29, 1869.

Joint Resolution of the National Council, Declaring Ezekiel Starr as Judge, and Rufus Adair as Sheriff, of Sequoyah District, according to the Election held in said District, on the First Monday in August, 1869.

Be it Resolved by the National Council, That Ezekiel Starr be, and he is hereby, declared to have been duly elected, at the last regular election, in Sequoyah District, held on the first Monday in August last, as Judge of [the] said District [Court]. And that Rufus Adair be, and he is hereby, declared to have been duly elected as Sheriff of said District. And the Principal Chief is hereby authorized to issue their Commissions accordingly.

Approved: LEWIS DOWNING,
Principal Chief of the Cherokee Nation.
Tahlequah, C. N., November 20, 1869.

A Joint Resolution of the National Council, Granting a License to Trade, to Joseph Thompson.

Resolved by the National Council, That Joseph Thompson, a citizen of the Cherokee Nation, be, and he is hereby, privileged to Trade in Merchandise generally, at the Mouth of Coon Creek, on Caney, in Coo-wee-scoo-wee District, C. N. He complying with the requirements of an Act of the National Council, dated November 7, 1866, regulating trade, &c.

Approved: LEWIS DOWNING,
Principal Chief of the Cherokee Nation.
Tahlequah, C. N., November 22, 1869.

Resolution Granting License to Trade.

Resolved, by the National Council, That permission is hereby granted to J. M. Bryan, Dennis Bushyhead, and William Percivil, citizens of the Cherokee Nation, to transact a general Mercantile Business at Fort Gibson, C. N., under the style of J. M. Bryan & Co.; they complying with the provisions of the Act regulating trade, dated November 7, 1866.

Approved: LEWIS DOWNING,
Principal Chief of the Cherokee Nation.
Tahlequah, C. N. November 27, 1869.

Resolution to Adjourn.

Resolved by the National Council, That the Senate and Council adjourn on Tuesday, 30th instant, at 4 o'clock, P. M.

Approved: LEWIS DOWNING,
Principal Chief of the Cherokee Nation.
Tahlequah, C. N., November 27, 1869.

Resolution in Regard to the Atlantic and Pacific Railroad.

WHEREAS, The Atlantic and Pacific Railroad Company, through Francis B. Hayes, its President, has transmitted a Memorial for the consideration of the Cherokee National Council, dated 22d October, 1869, in which it is represented that the Congress of the United States has granted to said Railroad Company, every Alternate Section of Public Land, not Mineral, designated by odd numbers, to the amount of Twenty Alternate Sections per Mile, on each side of said Railroad Line, as said Company may adopt. And,

WHEREAS, It is represented that the Congress of the United States has authorized the said Company to apply for, and accept to its own use, any grant, donations, loan, power, franchise, aid or assistance, from any Indian Tribe, subject to the approval of the President of the United States. And,

WHEREAS, In said Memorial, the National Council is required to cede and grant to the said Atlantic and Pacific Railroad Company, all the lands and other advantages, which, under and by said act of the United States, have agreed should be granted, so far as the same is applicable to the Cherokee Nation, and its lands and property, and also to grant other aid, in money or property, to facilitate the completion of said Road.

Now, THEREFORE, after a full and careful consideration of the said Memorial,

Be it Resolved by the Senate and Council of the Cherokee Nation, in National Council Convened, That the several requests made in said Memorial, for a grant of land, aid, and assistance in money, to facilitate the building of said Road, are hereby respectfully declined, and deemed contrary to our Treaty of 1866 with the Government of the United States, and the fixed policy of our people in relation to the ownership of land in the Cherokee Nation, by citizens of the United States, or Corporations composed of citizens of the United States.

Resolved, further, That a copy of these Resolutions be furnished Francis B. Hayes, President of the Atlantic and Pacific Railroad Company; one copy to the Secretary of the Interior; and one copy to the Commissioner of Indian Affairs.

Approved: LEWIS DOWNING,

Principal Chief of the Cherokee Nation.

Tahlequah, C. N., November 29, 1869.

ACTS AND JOINT RESOLUTIONS

OF THE

NATIONAL COUNCIL, IN EXTRA SESSION,

COMMENCING 1ST DECEMBER, 1869.

PROCLAMATION.

WHEREAS, It appears that the National Council has not been able, at its Regular Session, of 1869, to complete the transaction of business before it, whereby the public interests are jeopardized, and much important public business is left undone, which the public interest demands should be promptly attended to, thereby making the present an extraordinary occasion; and,

WHEREAS, The Principal Chief is authorized, by the Constitution, to convene the National Council, at the Seat of Government, on extraordinary occasions—and deeming this to be one—therefore,

I, LEWIS DOWNING, Principal Chief of the Cherokee Nation, issue this, my Proclamation, calling upon the several Members of the Senate and Council, of the several Districts of the Nation, to meet, and assemble in National Council, at the Seat of Government, at 10 o'clock, A. M., on the 1st day of December, 1869.

In witness whereof, I have hereunto set my hand and seal, at the Executive Department of the Cherokee Nation, in the Town of Tahlequah, C. N., on the 30th day of November, 1869.

{ L.S. } LEWIS DOWNING,
Principal Chief of the Cherokee Nation.

W. L. G. MILLER, *Private Secretary.*

An Act Admitting Betsy Ann Sullivan, and Children, to Citizenship in the Cherokee Nation.

Be it enacted by the National Council, That Betsy Ann Sullivan, a Cherokee by birth, and her seven children, viz: James, Robert, Andrew, William Perry, Willis Strawberry, Jeff. Davis, and Annie, be, and they are hereby, admitted to the rights and privileges of Citizenship in the Cherokee Nation.

Received, and Approved, 1st December, 1869.

LEWIS DOWNING,
Principal Chief of the Cherokee Nation.

Tahlequah, C. N., November 19, 1869.

An Act to Build a Court House in Saline District.

Be it enacted by the National Council, That the place of holding Courts in Saline District be, and is hereby, established on Little Spring Creek, at or near the residence of Samuel Smith; and that there be appropriated out of the Public Funds, not otherwise appropriated, the sum of Three Hundred Dollars, for the purpose of building a comfortable and commodious Court House at said point, in accordance with the provisions of this Act; and the District Judge and Sheriff of said District be, and are hereby, authorized, and it is made their duty, to employ some suitable person, or persons, to build said Court House, and to report the same to the National Council ensuing.

Approved, when presented, on the 2nd December, 1869.

LEWIS DOWNING,
Principal Chief of the Cherokee Nation.

Tahlequah, C. N., November 30, 1869.

Act of the National Council, Requiring the Principal Chief to Call Upon the United States Agent for the Cherokees, to Protest Against the Unlawful Acts of Pretended or Real U. S. Marshals, or their Deputies, in the Cherokee Nation.

WHEREAS, From time to time, heretofore, and at present, various unscrupulous persons, citizens of the United States, styling themselves as "Deputy Marshals" of the United States Court, of the Western District of Arkansas, have passed, and are passing, through the Cherokee Country, and through the Indian Territory, and without Warrants, as provided under the Constitution of the United States, and against the Law known as the "Law Regulating Trade and Intercourse between the Government and the Indian Tribes," and contrary to our Treaty stipulations with the United States Government; and

WHEREAS, Such persons have committed, and are still committing, numerous depredations upon the persons and property of the Cherokees,—1st, in robbing them of their property; 2d, in maltreating and abusing their persons, including those of helpless women and children, and in that condition have deprived them of their liberties, and dragged them far away from their homes, and incarcerated them in dungeons; therefore,

Be it enacted by the National Council, That the Principal Chief be, and he is hereby, authorized and required, at his earliest convenience, to call upon the United States Cherokee Agent, to protest, in behalf of the Cherokees, before the proper authorities of the United States, against the said conduct of the said lawless persons; and, in that connection, to call upon His Excellency, the President of the United States, for protection to the Cherokees, according to the solemn faith of the Government, pledged by Treaty stipulations.

Approved: LEWIS DOWNING,
Principal Chief of the Cherokee Nation.

Tahlequah, C. N., December 2, 1869.

An Act for Taking a Census of the Cherokee Nation, in the Year 1870; and Conferring Power upon the Supreme Court to Try and Determine Cases of Doubtful Citizenship at an Extra Term.

SECTION 1. *Be it enacted by the National Council*, That two expert and responsible persons, to be appointed by the Principal Chief, [in each District], and who shall be residents of the District from which they are appointed, be, and they are hereby, directed and authorized to take the Census of their respective Districts, between the 1st day of March and the 1st day of September, 1870, and make full and certified Returns thereof to the Principal Chief, on or before the 1st day of October, of said year. The said Census takers, before entering upon the duty hereby assigned them, shall take an oath, for the full, impartial, and correct perperformance of the same, as hereinafter defined.

SEC. 2. That it shall be the duty of said Census takers to take a full and complete Return of all persons found residing or sojourning within the limits of their respective Districts, at the time of making the Enumeration, as required by the foregoing section. And said Returns shall show the names of all heads of families; the names of all males above the age of eighteen [years]; the names of all females above the age of eighteen years; the names of all males under the age of eighteen years; the names, sex, and ages of all orphans, under sixteen years; the names of all whites, entitled by law to citizenship, within the ages above specified; the names of whites not so entitled; the names of all colored persons, entitled by law to citizenship, within said ages; and the names of all such persons not so entitled; and the names of all Indians not so entitled.

SEC. 3. That it shall be the duty of the Principal Chief to cause ruled blanks to be prepared, of a suitable and convenient form, and furnished to said Census takers, for the purpose of making the Enumeration herein provided for; and said Census takers shall be allowed Three Dollars per day while engaged in the performance of the duties hereinbefore imposed upon them.

SEC. 4. That it shall be the duty of the Principal Chief

to cause a Summary of the Returns of said Census to be prepared and laid before the National Council, together with the full Returns of the same, at the beginning of the Annual Session thereof in 1870. And which Returns shall serve as the basis for apportioning the representation of the several Districts of the Cherokee Nation, in the National Council, in accordance with the Amendments to the Constitution, dated November 28, 1866.

SEC. 5. That all persons, whose rights to citizenship in the Cherokee Nation shall be called in question, and who shall be reported by the persons authorized by this Act to take a Census of the Cherokee people, on the list of doubtful persons, shall be required to appear before the Supreme Court of the Cherokee Nation, at Tahlequah, on the 1st Monday in December, 1870, then and there to establish their rights to Citizenship in this Nation. And the said Supreme Court is hereby specially empowered to act as a Court of Commissioners on behalf of the Nation, for the hearing and determination of all cases of doubtful citizenship, which shall be reported to it by the Census takers, or by the Solicitors of the several Districts; and the decision of said Court shall be deemed final, and conclusive in the premises, as to the rights of said persons to citizenship in the Cherokee Nation. And the said Court shall cause a correct list of the names and ages of all persons whose rights they may confirm, and one of all those whose rights they may reject, to be placed on record in their office, and a copy of the same to be furnished to the Principal Chief, for the use of the Executive Office.

Approved, December 3d, 1869, the day of presentation.

LEWIS DOWNING,
Principal Chief of the Cherokee Nation.

Tahlequah, C. N., November 26, 1869.

An Act to Amend "An Act in Reference to Trade and Licensed Traders," Passed November 7, 1866.

Be it enacted by the National Council, That the Act

passed November 7th, 1866, Regulating Trade, be, and the same is hereby, so amended as to authorize and require the Treasurer of the Cherokee Nation to grant all Licenses to Cherokee Citizens to Trade in Goods, Wares, and Merchandise.

Approved, December 7, 1869.

LEWIS DOWNING.

Principal Chief of the Cherokee Nation.

Tahlequah, C. N., November 29th, 1869.

An Act for the Benefit of J. B. Jones.

Be it enacted by the National Council, That the Act passed November 23d, 1869, authorizing the Rev. J. B. Jones to Translate certain English Books into the Cherokee Language, be, and the same is hereby, so amended as to authorize the Principal Chief to issue to the said Jones, for his services, as aforesaid, his Warrants on the Treasury Quarterly.

Approved: LEWIS DOWNING,

Principal Chief of the Cherokee Nation.

Tahlequah, C. N., December 3, 1869.

An Act in Reference to Bounties and Pensions, Due Cherokees from the United States Government, for their Services in the United States Army, During the Late War.

Be it enacted by the National Council, That the United States Cherokee Agent, in connection with the Principal Chief of this Nation, be requested to adopt such means as will hereafter require the proper officer, or officers, of the United States Government, to pay out, in money, to all Cherokees, in person, or their legal representatives, all Bounty and Pensions now due, or that may be hereafter due them, on account of their service in the United States Army during the late War of the Rebellion.

Approved: LEWIS DOWNING,

Principal Chief of the Cherokee Nation.

Tahlequah, C. N., December 2, 1869.

An Act Making an Appropriation for the Repairing of the Male and Female Seminaries.

Be it enacted by the National Council, That the sum of Three Thousand Two Hundred and Forty Dollars be, and the same is hereby, appropriated, out of the School Fund, not otherwise appropriated, for the repair of the Male and Female Seminaries; and the Principal Chief is hereby authorized to draw Warrants for the same.

Be it further enacted, That the Principal Chief is hereby authorized to employ some suitable mechanic to repair said Seminaries, so as to preserve them from any further destruction, including repairs upon the roofs, cornices, floors, and windows, and enclosing with shutters or blinds the cupolas of both buildings.

Be it further enacted, That the Principal Chief be authorized to place some responsible person, or family, in charge of said Seminary Buildings, and who shall be required and empowered to preserve said buildings and premises from intrusions and trespass.

Approved: LEWIS DOWNING,

Principal Chief of the Cherokee Nation.

Tahlequah, C. N., December 6, 1869.

An Act Changing [*the*] *Time of Holding the Circuit Court in Canadian District.*

Be it enacted by the National Council, That the Regular Term of the Circuit Court in Canadian District shall hereafter be held on the last Monday in April and August, in each year; and any business now pending, returnable to the first Monday in May, and all business continued from the last September Term of the Circuit Court, in said District, to the first Monday in May next, shall be tried at the Term above designated, to-wit: the last Monday in April, 1870.

Approved, December 9, 1869.

LEWIS DOWNING,
Principal Chief of the Cherokee Nation.
Tahlequah, C. N., November 29, 1869.

An Act Authorizing the Principal Chief to Appoint a Delegation.

WHEREAS, It is deemed expedient that a Delegation should be appointed to represent the interests of this Nation before the Government of the United States; therefore,

Be it enacted by the National Council, That there be appointed, in the manner provided for by the Constitution, a Delegation, to consist of five persons, who shall be authorized to proceed to Washington City, for the purpose of representing the Cherokee Nation, with such powers, and in relation to such subjects, as shall be hereafter bestowed upon them by the National Council.

Be it further enacted, That the Principal Chief be requested to accompany said Delegation.

Be it further enacted, That said Delegation shall be allowed Two Hundred Dollars each, for travelling expenses, and Seven Dollars per day, while necessarily absent on their Mission, in full for their services, and all other personal expenses; payable out of such appropriation as may be made for that purpose by the National Council.

Be it further enacted, That the sum of Seven Thousand Dollars, or so much thereof as may be necessary, including One Thousand Dollars for the use of the Principal Chief, be, and the same is hereby appropriated, to defray the expenses of said Delegation.

Approved: LEWIS DOWNING,
Principal Chief of the Cherokee Nation.
Tahlequah, C. N., December 9, 1869.

An Act to Amend the Act for Taking the Census of the Cherokee Nation in 1870.

Be it enacted by the National Council, That the Act providing for the taking of the Census of the Cherokee Nation, in the year 1870, be, and the same is hereby, so amended, that the Principal Chief be, and he is hereby, authorized to draw Warrants on the Treasurer, on the certified accounts of parties, for the purpose of defraying the expenses of "Ruled Blanks" for the use of the Census takers.

Approved: LEWIS DOWNING,
Principal Chief of the Cherokee Nation.
Tahlequah, C. N., December 9, 1869.

An Act for the Benefit of D. H. Ross.

Be it enacted by the National Council, That Daniel H. Ross be, and he is hereby, allowed to establish and confirm his rights to the following Lots and Improvements in the Town of Fort Gibson, before Messrs. W. L. G. Miller and F. A. Kerr, late Commissioners, within two months after the passage of this Act, in accordance with the Act dated Nov., 1868, to-wit:—The Lots and Buildings known as the Old Church Property, and the Lot and Buildings known as the Mackey Place. And the said Commissioners are hereby authorized to hear and act upon the claim of the said D. H. Ross, in accordance with the intention of this Act.

Approved: LEWIS DOWNING,
Principal Chief of the Cherokee Nation.
Tahlequah, C. N., December 11, 1869.

An Act to Procure a National Seal.

Be it enacted by the National Council, That the Principal Chief be, and he is hereby, authorized to procure a National Seal, for the use of the Cherokee Nation, to be used by the Principal Chief, and such Officer as may be designated by law, in the sealing of documents. And the expense of said Seal shall be paid out of any funds in the National Treasury, belonging to the National Fund, not otherwise appropriated; and the Principal Chief is authorized to draw Warrants accordingly.

Be it further enacted, That the said Seal shall bear the following device, viz:—In the centre thereof there shall be a seven-pointed star, surrounded with a wreath of oak leaves, and in the margin of said Seal shall be the words: "Seal of the Cherokee Nation," "Sept. 6th, 1839," and the following Cherokee characters: ᏣᎳᎩ ᎠᏰᎵ; and the said Seal shall be one and a half inches in diameter.

Approved: LEWIS DOWNING,
Principal Chief of the Cherokee Nation.
Tahlequah, C. N., December 11, 1869.

An Act for the Relief of Jennie Watts.

Be it enacted by the National Council, That the bonds of matrimony heretofore existing between Jennie Watts (formerly Jennie Tally) and Charles Watts, be, and are hereby, dissolved and annulled, and a full and free divorce granted to the said Jennie Watts, from the said Charles Watts.

Approved: LEWIS DOWNING,
Principal Chief of the Cherokee Nation.
Tahlequah, C. N., December 13, 1869.

An Act Creating Ten Additional Public Schools.

Be it enacted by the National Council, That from and after the expiration of the present Session of the Public Schools there be established Ten additional Public Schools, to be located as follows, to-wit:

1. One at or near Muddy Springs, Flint District.

2. One on the line between Illinois and Sequoyah Districts, near Richard Benge's, in Illinois District.

3. One at or near Locust Grove, in Saline District.

4. One at or near Black Jack Grove, in Canadian District.

5. One on the line between Illinois and Tahlequah Districts, near William Green's, in Illinois District.

6. One at or near Peggy Woodall's, in Tahlequah District.

7. One at or near John Sarcoxie's, in Coo-wee-scoo-wee District.

8. One at or near Arch. Ballard's, Delaware District.

9. One at or near Wilson Sitting Down's, Sequoyah District.

10. One at or near George Whitmire's, Going Snake District.

Provided, That at the said localities there shall be comfortable School-houses built by the citizens of their respective vicinities, previous to tbe date of this Act going into effect.

Be it further enacted, That the Colored Schools, previously provided for by Law, and now in operation at Tahlequah, and on Fourteen Mile Creek, in Tahlequah District, be, and they are hereby, located at or near their present localities.

Be it further enacted, That the provisions of the Act making an Appropriation for the support of the Public Schools for the year 1869–70, which authorized the employment of Assistant Teachers for the Public Schools at Fort Gibson, Tahlequah, and Baptist Mission, and appropriates the sum of Nine Hundred Dollars for their pay, be, and the same is hereby, repealed.

Tahlequah, C. N., December 10, 1869.

ARCH. SCRAPER,
President of Senate.

GEO. W. JOHNSON,
Clerk of Senate.

Concurred, with the following changes, to-wit:—In place of the name of "Arch. Ballard," insert Dick Old Fields;

in place of "Locust Grove," insert Falling Pot; and in place of "William Green," insert John Ratling Gourd.

STAND WHIRLWIND,
Speaker of Council.

C. N. Vann,
Clerk of Council.

Amendment concurred in:

ARCH. SCRAPER,
President of Senate.

Geo. W. Johnson,
Clerk of Senate.

Approved: LEWIS DOWNING,
Principal Chief of the Cherokee Nation.

Tahlequah, C. N., December 13, 1869.

An Act in Relation to the Capitol Building.

Be it enacted by the National Council, That the Committee entrusted with the erection of the Building for the Capitol be authorized and directed to settle with Charles Cranwell, Contractor, for the Masonry and Brick Work done by him, agreeably to the terms of his Contract, including the openings not named in the Contract, and omitting the Painting of said Building; and also to cause to be issued to him Warrants, in payment for amount found to be due him, and which, together with those already drawn in his favor, shall be payable on presentation to the Treasurer of the Nation.

Be it further enacted, That the Building Committee be authorized to contract for the Plastering of said Building, to be done as early in the ensuing season as the weather will allow; and that James S. Price, Contractor for Carpenter Work, be allowed until the 1st day of July, he renewing his Bond, with Surety, for the performance of his Contract, and to complete his work. And that he be relieved as a member of the Building Committee, and John Lynch Adair be appointed hereby in his place.

Be it further enacted, That the Building Committee be authorized to cause said Capitol Building to be painted in an appropriate manner, of some suitable solid colors, and the Principal Chief is hereby authorized to pay for the same out of the Fund already appropriated for said Building.

Be it further enacted, That Johnson Foreman and Allen Ross, of the Senate, and Jesse Baldridge and Charles Drew, of the Council, be, and they are hereby, appointed a Joint Committee, on behalf of the National Council, with authority to cause said Building to be appropriately and substantially furnished, with Chairs, Tables, Stoves, &c., and to have the same in readiness to be occupied on the meeting of the next Annual Session of the National Council. And the sum of Two Thousand Dollars, or so much thereof as may be necessary, is hereby appropriated to defray the expenses thus incurred.

Be it further enacted, That the Keeper of the Public Buildings be directed to cause the Contractor to enclose the Public Square, to complete the same in a substantial manner, according to his contract, within two months from the date hereof. And that he be further authorized to sell, to the highest bidder, at public sale, after publicly advertising the same twenty days, the Printing Office, and Lot on which it stands, and also the two Log Cabins within the Public Square, and which latter buildings shall be removed within ten days after their sale, or be re-sold under the terms of the authority herein conferred upon the Keeper of the Public Buildings. The terms of the sale, for the Lot and Buildings sold under this section, shall be Cash or National Warrants, payable one-half at time of sale, and the other half within six months after date.

Approved: LEWIS DOWNING,

Principal Chief of the Cherokee Nation.

Tahlequah, C. N., December 13, 1869.

An Act in Relation to Stone Coal.

Be it enacted by the National Council, That the Principal Chief be, and he is hereby, authorized to lease out any Coal Mine, or Mines, in the Cherokee Nation, to any Cherokee, or to any Company of Citizens of the Cherokee Nation, during the pleasure of the National Council, upon the terms and conditions hereinafter provided. And said Coal Mine, or Mines, so leased, shall be as accurately described as practicable in the said lease.

Be it further enacted, That any person or Company, leasing a Mine, or Mines, of Coal, as above provided, shall be required to keep an account of all Coal dug and sold by them, and pay to the Sheriff, on the 1st of May and October, five per cent. tax upon the proceeds of all Coal sold, from the working of said Coal Mines. *Provided*, The Sheriff receiving the said tax shall first put the person, or persons, paying the same, on oath, as to the correctness of said tax.

Be it further enacted, That any Cherokee, or Company of Cherokee Citizens, as above provided, who may wish to obtain a lease of any Coal Mine, or Mines, shall first put on file in the Executive Office, a Bond for the sum of One Thousand Dollars, with good security, conditioned upon the payment of said tax, in accordance with this Act.

Be it further enacted, That nothing in this Act shall be so construed as to prevent any Cherokee from digging Coal for his own use, and not for sale, without paying said tax.

Be it further enacted, That any person who shall dig Coal, for the purpose of selling the same, or [who] shall sell Coal outside of the Cherokee Nation, without the authority of a lease from the Principal Chief, as above provided, shall be fined in the sum of Fifty Dollars for each offence; one-half to go to the Solicitor of the District who prosecutes the case, and the other half to the National Treasury. *Provided*, That no such Company (as is provided for in this Act), or any member thereof, shall obtain a lease, or be interested in more than one Coal Mine at the same time, and the lease to such Mine, so described, shall not exceed one-half mile square.

Approved: LEWIS DOWNING,

Principal Chief of the Cherokee Nation.

Tahlequah, C. N., December 14, 1869.

An Act Re-Admitting the Persons Therein Named to Citizenship.

Be it enacted by the National Council, That Mary Ann

Grey, and children; Logan H. Duncan, Penelope C. Duncan, and Granville Craig; Martha Maars, and children; David B. McDaniel, and family; Lydia Quinton, Joseph Kelly, Moses Crittenden, Isaac Howel, William Beck, John Quinton, and Levi Robins, and their families, who are Cherokees, be, and they are hereby, re-admitted to Citizenship in this Nation.

Be it further enacted, That Hannah B. Hitchcock, widow of Dr. D. D. Hitchcock, and daughter of the late Rev'd Samuel A. Worcester, be, and she is hereby, re-admitted to Citizenship in this Nation.

ARCH. SCRAPER,
President of the Senate.

Geo. W. Johnson,
Clerk of the Senate.

This Act was concurred in, by erasing the name of Hannah B. Hitchcock.

STAND WHIRLWIND,
Speaker of Council.

Stephen Foreman,
Clerk of Council.

Concur in amendment.

ARCH. SCRAPER,
President of the Senate.

Geo. W. Johnson,
Clerk of the Senate.

Approved: LEWIS DOWNING.
Principal Chief of the Cherokee Nation.
Tahlequah, C. N., December 15, 1869.

An Act Granting the Use of the Town Lots Herein Named.

Be it enacted by the National Council, That the Principal Chief be, and he is hereby, authorized to grant the use of one Lot each, in the Town of Fort Gibson, belonging to the Cherokee Nation, to the Public Schools located at that place.

Approved: LEWIS DOWNING,
Principal Chief of the Cherokee Nation.
Tahlequah, C. N., December 11, 1869.

An Act to Instruct the Delegation.

WHEREAS, The National Council, having determined by enactment dated the 9th inst., that it was expedient to authorize the appointment of a Delegation, to consist of the Principal Chief and five persons, to proceed to Washington City, for the purpose of transacting with the Government of the United States such business of a public character as might be entrusted to their care; and,

WHEREAS, In pursuance of the said authority, the Principal Chief, by and with the advice and consent of the Senate of the Cherokee Nation, has appointed Samuel Smith, J. P. Davis, Archibald Scraper, Clement N. Vann, and S. H. Benge, to compose said Delegation; now, therefore,

Be it enacted by the National Council, That the before named Lewis Downing, Principal Chief, Samuel Smith, J. P. Davis, Archibald Scraper, Clement N. Vann, and S. H. Benge, be, and they are hereby, appointed and constituted a Delegation, to proceed to Washington City, for the purpose, and with the authority, of representing the interests of the Cherokee Nation, before the Government of the United States.

Be it further enacted, That the said Delegation be invested with full and ample powers, to adjust, by Treaty, or otherwise, all questions involving the interests of the Cherokee Nation, existing by Treaty, or in any other way growing out of our relations with the United States, excepting only that said Delegation shall have no power or authority whatever, (to impair the rights, privileges and immunities, guarantied to the Cherokee Nation, by any Treaty now in force), to limit, curtail, or dispose of the domain of the Cherokee Nation, East of 96 deg. West longitude, and South of the 37th deg. North latitude; nor to admit or incorporate, without the approval of the National Council, any Indians within the limits of the Cherokee Country, East of 96 deg. West longitude; nor to subscribe to the Stock of any Company or Corporation, outside of this Nation, and independent of its authority and jurisdiction, desiring to run a Railroad through the Cherokee Nation; nor to invest the Funds and Securities of the Nation, in the Bonds of any such Company or Corporation; nor to make any grants of Land to the same, other than has been made by the 11th Article of the Treaty of 11th August, 1866—(it being the purpose and intention of the National Council, hereby to withhold from the said Delegation any and all power or authority to bind the Cherokee Nation, or complicate its interests in any way with any Railroad Company or Corporation in existence, or that may be created beyond the limits of this Nation, and independent of its authority and jurisdiction.)

Be it further enacted, That the before named Delegation be instructed to obtain from Congress authority to construct the Railroads through the Cherokee Nation, contemplated by the 11th Article of the Treaty of 11th August, 1866, between the United States and the Cherokee Nation, by such Company as may be organized by the Cherokee Nation, and to ask the aid of the Government of the United States in constructing the same, by granting such subsidy as may be agreed upon between the United States and the said Delegation, and not inconsistent with these instructions.

Be it further enacted, That the said Delegation shall also ask the aid and co-operation of the Government in establishing an Industrial School within the limits of this Nation, for the education of such Orphan Children of Indian descent as may be admitted to its care and instruction, and upon such terms as may be agreed between the proper authorities of the Indian Bureau and the before named Delegation.

Be it further enacted, That the Principal Chief be, and he is hereby, authorized to fill any vacancy that may occur in said Delegation.

Be it further enacted, That the said Delegation be, and they are hereby, authorized to employ such Attorneys as they may deem necessary in the discharge of their duties.

ARCH. SCRAPER,
President of the Senate.

GEO. W. JOHNSON,
Clerk of the Senate.

Concurred in:

JOHN CHAMBERS,
Speaker of Council pro tem.

C. N. VANN,
Clerk of Council.

Amended, in the 2d Section, 9th line, by striking out all

the words from the word "whatever," in said line, to the word "to," in the 12th line; then insert in the 20th line the words "outside of this Nation, and independent of its authority and jurisdiction;" then strike out all from the figures "1866," 26th line.

ARCH. SCRAPER,
President of the Senate.

GEO. W. JOHNSON,
Clerk of the Senate.

Concurred in above Amendment, as set forth in the above lines.

STAND WHIRLWIND,
Speaker of Council.

S. FOREMAN,
Clerk of Council.

Approved: LEWIS DOWNING,
Principal Chief of the Cherokee Nation.
Tahlequah, C. N., December 16, 1869.

[NOTE BY THE PRINTER.—In the Amendment to the above Act, the numbers of the lines in which changes are made refer to the manuscript, and not the printed matter.]

An Act to Repeal An Act to Regulate the Issue of Permits to Hire Citizens of the United States.

Be it enacted by the National Council, That the Act entitled "An Act to Regulate the issue of Permits to hire Citizens of the United States," approved Nov. 22d, 1867, be, and the same is hereby, repealed. *Provided*, That this Act shall not be deemed to annul Permits already issued under said Act.

Approved: LEWIS DOWNING,
Principal Chief of the Cherokee Nation.
Tahlequah, C. N., December 15, 1869.

An Act for the Protection of the Public Domain.

Be it enacted by the National Council, That any Citizen, or Company of Citizens of this Nation, who may desire to dispose of Sawed Lumber to Citizens of the United States, either in or outside of this Nation, shall, before doing so, obtain a License for that purpose from the Treasurer of the Cherokee Nation, and shall file a Bond before him, with good security, in the penal sum of Five Thousand Dollars, conditioned upon a compliance with the requirements of this Act, hereinafter expressed, to dispose of Sawed Lumber; and the sale of all other Timber to such persons, and its conveyance beyond the limits of this Nation, is hereby expressly declared to be unlawful; and any person convicted thereof, shall be punished, as hereinafter provided.

1st. Such person, or persons, so using or disposing of Sawed Lumber, shall report, in April and October, in each year, on oath, the amount of funds received by them, by such disposition, and shall, at the same time, pay into the Treasury fifteen per centum on the amounts reported.

2d. Any person, or persons, who may violate this Act, shall, in addition to forfeiting the said Bond for the benefit of the Treasury of the Nation, be deemed guilty of a high misdemeanor, and on conviction thereof before the proper Court of the District in which such offence may be committed, shall be fined not less than One Hundred, nor exceeding Five Hundred Dollars, at the discretion of the Court.

3d. Such person, or persons, so disposing of Lumber, shall be required to make Quarterly Reports to the Sheriffs of their respective Districts, on oath, of all amounts received by them, for all Lumber disposed of; and it shall be the duty of the said Sheriffs to report the said amounts to the Treasurer of the Nation, on the 1st Monday in November, in each year.

Be it further enacted, That it shall be the duty of the several Solicitors of this Nation to prosecute all persons violating this Act; and should any Solicitor fail to prosecute any such offenders he shall be subject to a fine for every such failure, for the benefit of the Treasury of the Nation, in a sum of not less than Fifty Dollars, nor exceeding One Hundred Dollars, to be deducted from his salary.

Be it further enacted, That this Act shall not be so construed as to authorize any person to obtain or use Timber within one-fourth of a mile of the occupied premises of any Citizen of this Nation, without the consent of such Citizen; nor shall it be construed so as to deny the right of the United States to use Timber for various purposes, as provided for by Treaty stipulations between the Cherokee Nation and the United States; nor to authorize or allow any individual or Company to hold or occupy, or be interested in more than one claim, in any Pinery, or other forest, at the same time, and in accordance with the Laws of this Nation, regulating settlements on the Public Domain.

Approved: LEWIS DOWNING,
Principal Chief of the Cherokee Nation.
Tahlequah, C. N., December 17, 1869.

Resolution Authorizing T. B. Wolfe to Trade.

Resolved by the National Council, That Thomas B. Wolfe be, and he is hereby, authorized and privileged to continue in the Mercantile Business in the Town of Tahlequah, C. N. *Provided*, That he comply with the Act of November, 1866, Regulating Trade in the Cherokee Nation.

Approved: LEWIS DOWNING,
Principal Chief of the Cherokee Nation.
Tahlequah, C. N. November 27, 1869.

Resolution to Adjourn.

Be it Resolved by the National Council, That the National Council Adjourn its present Called Session on Wednesday next, the 15th inst., 1869, at 10 o'clock, A. M.

Approved: LEWIS DOWNING,
Principal Chief of the Cherokee Nation.
Tahlequah, C. N., December 10, 1869.

Joint Resolution of the National Council, in Regard to the North Carolina Cherokees.

WHEREAS, Sundry Petitions have been transmitted to the

National Council, by the "North Carolina Cherokees," from which it appears that the said Cherokees, (or a portion of them), are desirous of removing, and becoming members of the Cherokee Nation; and,

WHEREAS, The Principal Chief has transmitted a communication to the National Council, enclosing one from the Commissioner of Indian Affairs, from which it appears that the Hon. Commissioner desires to know the wishes of the Cherokee Nation, in reference to the removal of the North Carolina Indians; therefore,

Be it Resolved by the National Council, That the Principal Chief be, and he is hereby, authorized to inform the Hon. Commissioner of Indian Affairs of the willingness of the Cherokee Nation to receive the said "North Carolina Cherokees" into the Cherokee Nation. *Provided*, That they remove without any expense to the Treasury of the Cherokee Nation. And, *Provided*, *further*, That these Resolutions shall not be so construed as to admit any Cherokee rights or benefits *now* claimed, or heretofore claimed by the said "North Carolina Cherokees," until they shall have removed West, and been identified as Citizens of the Cherokee Nation.

Be it further resolved, That the Principal Chief be, and he is hereby, authorized to notify the said "North Carolina Cherokees" of the willingness of the Cherokee Nation to receive them as Citizens of the Cherokee Nation, upon the terms herein before expressed.

Approved: LEWIS DOWNING,

Principal Chief of the Cherokee Nation.

Tahlequah, C. N., December 10, 1869.

Resolution Changing Time of Adjournment.

Resolved by the Senate and Council of the Cherokee Nation, That the National Council adjourn *sine die* on Saturday, the 18th instant, at 10 o'clock, A. M., and the Resolution fixing Wednesday, the 15th instant, as the day of adjournment of the National Council, is hereby repealed.

Approved: LEWIS DOWNING,

Principal Chief of the Cherokee Nation.

Tahlequah, C. N., December 14, 1869.

Resolution Granting a License to Trade to G. A. Meyer, a Citizen of the United States.

Resolved, by the National Council, That the approval of the National Council, according to the 8th Article of the Cherokee Treaty of 1866, is hereby given to the United States Agent to grant a License to Trade, in "Goods, Wares, and Merchandise," to G. A. Meyer & Co., a Citizen of the United States, according to the "Laws Regulating Trade and Intercourse with the Indian Tribes."

Approved: LEWIS DOWNING,
Principal Chief of the Cherokee Nation.
Tahlequah, C. N., December 15, 1869.

This is to Certify, That the Act in relation to Stone Coal, approved December 14, 1869; the Act to amend an Act in relation to Tax on Stock passing through and grazing in the Cherokee Country, approved November 25, 1869; and an Act for the Protection of the Public Domain, approved December 17, 1869—have been published for Ninety Days, in the *Chetopa Advance*, a Newspaper published in Kansas, and the Editor directed to furnish two copies of the same to each Sheriff in the Nation.

JAMES VANN,
Acting Principal Chief of the Cherokee Nation.
W. L. G. MILLER, *Secretary.*
Tahlequah, C. N., March 26, 1870.

INDEX.

PAGE

Act of Union between the Eastern and Western Cherokees, - - - - - - - - - - 3
Constitution of the Cherokee Nation, - - - - 5
Preamble and Resolution submitting to the people Amendments to the Constitution, - - 17
Amendments to Articles 1st and 3d, - - - - 18
Amendments to Article 5th, - - - - - - 20
Additional Article, No. 7, - - - - - - - 20
Amendments to the Constitution approved by the people, 21
Proclamation of the Principal Chief, promulgating Amendments to the Constitution, - - - - 21
Resolution in relation to the postponement of opening Election Returns, - - - - - - - 23
An Act making appropriations for special services, &c. 24
An Act making an appropriation for the benefit of Martin McCoy, James Trott, and Joseph Coody, - 24
An Act in reference to Delawares and Osages, - - 25
An Act creating a commission to investigate claims to town lots, buildings, &c., in Fort Gibson and Tahlequah, - - - - - - - - - - 26
An Act approving agreement with Munsee Indians, - 28
An Act removing Public School from White Springs to the mouth of Dog Creek, - - - - - 29
An Act repealing an Act authorizing persons to move into the Cherokee Nation, - - - - - 30
An Act authorizing the publication of Penal Laws, 30
An Act re-admitting John G. and Geo. W. Harnage, and families to citizenship, - - - - - - 32
An Act for the prompt payment of the expenses of the National Council, - - - - - - - - 32
An Act re-admitting William Harnage and family, 32

An Act to amend an Act relative to the Court House in Coo-wee-scoo-wee District, . - - - - 33
An Act for the benefit of Cynthia Pack, W. B. Taylor, and Lucy Man-Killer, - - - - - - 33
An Act making an appropriation in favor of Joseph Coody and the Treasurer, - - - - - 34
An Act for the relief of Judge E. Butler, - - 35
An Act granting citizenship to W. S. and R. B. Patton, 35
An Act to protect the School-house in Fort Gibson from sale, - - - - - - - - - - - 35
An Act providing for a National Printing Press, - 36
An Act to amend an Act entitled an Act to organize the Nation into eight Districts, &c., - - - - 37
An Act re-admitting Elijah Phillips, - - - - 38
Resolution to adjourn, - - - - - - - - 38
An Act for the benefit of A. W. Timberlake, - 39
An Act making an appropriation for the payment of a list of claims registered in 1868, - - - - 39
An Act making an appropriation to defray the expenses of the National Council, &c., at the Annual Session of 1868, - - - - - - - - 45
Appropriation for the pay of clerks, &c., for 1868, 48
An Act making appropriation for the support of Public Schools and Orphans for 1869, and to purchase books and stationery, - - - - - - 50
An Act making appropriation for the benefit of T. B. Wolfe and Company, &c., - - - - - 51
Resolution requiring the Principal Chief to furnish the National Council with Compiled Laws, - - 53
An Act authorizing the prompt payment of the expenses of the Extra Session of September, 1868, - 54
Resolution to furnish Superintendent Indian Affairs and Cherokee Agent with Compiled Laws, - - 54
Resolution granting the use of the Male Seminary to Superintendent Indian Affairs, - - - - 55
An Act to re-appoint a Delegation, - - - - - 55
An Act in relation to the election of members of the Grand Council, - - - - - - - - 55
An Act designating place of holding Courts in Delaware District, - - - - - - - - 57

An Act to re-establish Election Precincts in Coo-wee-scoo-wee District, - - - - - - 57
An Act to amend an Act for building a Capitol, - 58
Resolution setting time for adjournment, - - 59
An Act to instruct the Delegation, - - - - - 59
Appropriation to pay members of National Council and Executive Council, for Extra Session, Sept., 1868, 60
An Act requiring the Auditor to remain at the seat of government during the Session of 1869, &c., - 63
An Act to adopt I. N. Parker, - - - - - 64
An Act to provide for compiling and translating School Books, - - - - - - - 64
An Act to establish a National Newspaper, - - 65
An Act to amend an Act to regulate the issue of Pensions, - - - - - - - - 67
An Act to amend an Act in relation to Stock passing through the Nation, - - - - 67
An Act to repair Canadian Court-house, - - 69
An appropriation to complete the Court-house in Flint District, - - - - - - - 69
Special appropriation out of School Fund, - - 69
An appropriation for the support of the Public Schools, &c., for the year 1869–70, - - - - - 70
Resolution declaring officers elected in Sequoyah District, - - - - - - - - 72
Resolution granting license to trade to Joseph Thompson 72
Resolution granting license to trade to Bryan, Bushyhead & Percivil, - - - - - - 72
Resolution to adjourn, - - - - - - - - 73
Resolution in regard to the Atlantic & Pacific Railroad, 73
Proclamation of Principal Chief, calling an Extra Session of Council in 1869, - - - - - 75
An Act admitting Betsy Ann Sullivan and children to citizenship, - - - - - - - 76
An Act to build a Court-house in Saline District, - 76
An Act requiring Principal Chief to call for protection against U. S. Marshals, - - - - - - 77
An Act for taking the Census in 1870, - - - 78
An Act to amend an Act in reference to trade and licensed traders, - - - - - - - 79

An Act for the benefit of J. B. Jones, - - - 80
An Act in reference to Bounties and Pensions due from the United States, for service in the late war, - 80
An appropriation for repairing the Seminary buildings, 81
An Act changing the time of holding Circuit Court in Canadian District, - - - - - 81
An Act authorizing the Principal Chief to appoint a Delegation, - - - - - - - - 82
An Act to amend an Act for taking the Census in 1870, 83
An Act for the benefit of D. H. Ross, - - - - 83
An Act to procure a National Seal, - - - - 83
An Act divorcing Jennie Watts from Charles Watts, 84
An Act creating ten additional Schools, - - 84
An Act in relation to the Capitol building, - - 86
An Act in relation to Stone Coal, - - 87
An Act re-admitting the persons named to citizenship, 88
An Act granting the use of town lots to the Public Schools in Fort Gibson, - - - - - 89
An Act to instruct the Delegation, - - - - 90
An Act to repeal an Act regulating the issue of permits to hire citizens of the United States, - - 92
An Act for the protection of the public domain, - 92
An Act authorizing T. B. Wolfe to trade, - - 94
Resolution to adjourn, - - - - - - - - 94
Resolution in regard to North Carolina Cherokees, - 94
Resolution changing the time of adjournment, - - 95
Resolution granting license to trade to G. A. Meyer & Co., of the United States, - - - - - 96
Certificate of the Chief that certain penal laws have been published, - - - - - - - 96